"As a polyamorous parent, the question I get asked a lot is 'But what about the children?' Having a firsthand account by someone who lived, loved and learned in a polyamorous household is invaluable to any of us who raise children in the same environment. Bravo!"
    —Kevin A. Patterson, curator of Poly Role Models and
    author of *Love's Not Color Blind*

"If you're curious for a peek into what it's really like for kids growing up in a polyamorous family, look no further than this book. In this remarkably vulnerable piece of writing, Koe shares landmarks of their life as a means of answering the most frequently asked questions about poly youth. Highly recommended for anyone considering poly parenthood."
    —Cunning Minx, host of Polyamory Weekly and author
    of *Eight Things I Wish I'd Known About Polyamory*

"This is exactly what the world has been waiting for—a raw, honest perspective on what 'family' and 'tribe' can mean. Koe boldly shares their story and provides a helpful guide to navigating the complexities of polyamorous family structures. This is a must-read for everyone who chooses to live outside the box and create the best life for themselves!"
    —Eri Kardos, author of *Relationship Agreements*

"This autobiography of a young adult raised in a pagan, polyamorous extended family is full of information for parents and kids of all backgrounds. Useful ideas abound and lead the reader to question the traditional wisdom of our society."
    —David S. Hall, founding editor, *Electronic Journal of Human Sexuality*

"Koe Creation's delightful book *This Heart Holds Many* is perfect for anyone who has wondered how polyamorous families affect children, parents, and those Koe calls 'parent adjacent.' From the pregnant lady sandwich to the chaotic (mis)adventures of young love or the trials and triumphs of adulting, Koe guides readers through the life of a second-generation polyamorous person with charming candor."
— Dr. Elisabeth Sheff, author of *The Polyamorists Next Door* and *When Someone You Love is Polyamorous*, and editor of *Stories from the Polycule*

"An individual voice with a unique and fascinating story to tell."
— Barry Smiler, organizer of BmorePoly

"Koe Creation is such a force, and this book is a testament to their incredible impact on the world around them."
— Allena Gabosch, sex and relationships educator, activist, and author

"Imagine that a big tribal family from the 22nd century falls into our time and lands in Seattle, where they have to keep partly hidden from the normals. You're born into it and grow up through a rollicking kidhood, a moody, rebellious adolescence, then young-adult questing and brilliant maturity. All the while you hide your three moms and two dads from forces in the 'overculture' that may threaten them—while you become an ambassador from the 22nd century to many others. This fast-paced memoir grabs you like a piece of Heinlein's science fiction, while serving as a guide, a warning, an encouragement, and a wise teaching tool for families of every kind."
— Alan MacRobert, *Polyamory in the News*

This Heart Holds Many

This Heart Holds Many

My Life as the Nonbinary Millennial Child of a Polyamorous Family

Koe Creation
with a foreword by Dr. Elisabeth Sheff

Thorntree  Press

This Heart Holds Many
My Life as the Nonbinary Millennial Child of a Polyamorous Family
Copyright ©2019 by Koe Creation
Foreword copyright ©2019 by Elisabeth Sheff

Thorntree Press, LLC
P.O. Box 301231
Portland, OR 97294
press@thorntreepress.com

Thorntree Press's activities take place on traditional and ancestral lands of the Coast Salish people, including the Chinook, Musqueam, Squamish and Tsleil-Waututh nations.

Cover photo ©2016 by Rachel Saudek
Cover design by Brianna Harden
Interior design by Jeff Werner
Polycule illustration ©2018 Rowdy Ferret Designs
Developmental editing by Kari Castor and Michelle Lingo
Copy-editing by Roma Ilnyckyj
Proofreading by Hazel Boydell

Library of Congress Cataloging-in-Publication Data

Names: Creation, Koe, author.
Title: This heart holds many : my life as the nonbinary millennial child of
    a polyamorous family / Koe Creation ; foreword by Dr. Elisabeth Sheff.
Description: Portland, OR : Thorntree Press, [2019] |
Identifiers: LCCN 2018034919 (print) | LCCN 2018037127 (ebook) |
    ISBN 9781944934736 (epub) | ISBN 9781944934743 (mobipocket) |
    ISBN 9781944934750 (pdf) | ISBN 9781944934729 (softcover)
Subjects: LCSH: Creation, Koe. | Non-monogamous relationships--United States.
    | Group marriage--United States. | Families--United States.
    | Sexual minorities' families--United States. | Gender-
    nonconforming people--United States--Biography.
Classification: LCC HQ980.5.U5 (ebook) |
    LCC HQ980.5.U5 C74 2019 (print) | DDC 306.84/23--dc23
LC record available at https://lccn.loc.gov/2018034919

10 9 8 7 6 5 4 3 2 1

Printed in the United States of America on acid-free paper that is certified to the Forest Stewardship Council® standards.

To Ember Johnston, 1998–2018, for being
the guiding light to so many people who were
looking for permission to be themselves.
I love you and will always keep a lookout just
beyond the horizon, second star to the right.

"If anyone has ever told you that you are anything less than a work of art, they lied."
—Blyss Enns

Contents

Foreword

When I began studying polyamory in 1996, hardly anyone had heard of it. Because it was novel, and I was the only one in the United States studying it at the time, I was often invited to speak for classes and conferences about my findings. At these events I would ask people in the audience to raise their hands if they had heard of polyamory. For the first 10 years, hardly anyone raised their hands—certainly less than a quarter. Then, in the mid-2000s, I began to notice a steady increase in the number of raised hands, and I started asking people where they had heard about polyamory. All of them said they had first heard about it on the Internet, or from a friend who had heard about it on the Internet and sent them a link. Now, ten years later, I hardly ever ask that question anymore, because most of my audience has already heard of polyamory and is coming to the event to learn more.

Based on the skyrocketing Google search rates for terms like *polyamory* and *monogamish*, many people are interested in what happens in consensually non-monogamous relationships. Reality television producers contact me regularly to ask me to help find polyamorous families with children who will appear in a reality television show. At first I used to put call after call out to the online polyamorous community to ask if anyone wanted to participate, and for one producer, I even contacted some of my respondents personally. All of them said no, and none of the families in the polysphere on the Internet ever wanted to volunteer for the reality shows.

After a while, I stopped asking if people in polyamorous families would volunteer for reality television and instead asked them why they did not want to participate. Folks in poly-amorous families responded that they did not want to expose themselves, their families, and especially their kids to the kind of scrutiny and (too often vicious) social media attention that comes with being on reality television. Some people who had gone on television shows had very negative experiences with accusatory audience members and hosts who wanted salacious details at the expense of an accurate image of polyamorous families. My own experience being on the short-lived reboot of *The Ricki Lake Show* was rather negative: When the producers interviewed me on the phone, they asked a lot of questions about my research, and I thought they would introduce me as Dr. Sheff, a sociologist who researches polyamory. Instead, when I appeared on camera, the screen beneath me read "Eli, whose marriage was destroyed by polyamory." They eliminated virtually everything I said from the final show, I assume because it was not what they wanted to hear.

A few people who have been out on TV have had great experiences, especially with Lisa Ling's *Our America*. Over the last two decades, brave people have talked about their lives as polyamorists on television and, far more often, in print media interviews, which has given this current explosion of interest in consensual non-monogamies a more realistic image of poly folks. Families, and especially people raised in polyamorous families, have been most reluctant to expose themselves to the media. On the one hand, polyamorous folks fear that coming out on national television could make them lose their jobs, housing, custody of their kids, or relationships with their extended families. Polyamorous parents' biggest fear is that their kids will suffer the consequences with peers. One parent told me, "High school is hard enough as it is, and I'm gonna add fuel to that fire by talking about my two husbands on TV? I don't think so."

On the other hand, silence does not equal death for poly-amorous folks the way it did for the gay men who coined that phrase at the height of the 1980s AIDS epidemic. In fact, poly families can often blend in with their neighbors as people with a lot of friends or divorced families who get along well. There is nothing pushing these families to come out, and the consequences for coming out can be dangerous, so it is no surprise that most people in polyamorous families go about their lives quietly avoiding the media spotlight.

But the rising public awareness of polyamory, coupled with polyamorous families' reluctance to talk about their lives in public, has created a vast interest in these families with hardly any information. Into this gap comes Koe Creation's *This Heart Holds Many*: the first ever memoir about growing up in a polyamorous family. This delightful book is required reading for anyone who has wondered how polyamorous families affect children, parents and those Koe calls "parent adjacent." In a rare peek into the life of a "polykid" raised by five parents, Koe offers anecdotes from their life with a polytribe. From the pregnant-lady sandwich to the chaotic (mis)adventures of young love or the trials and triumphs of adulting, Koe guides readers through the life of a second-generation polyamorous person with charming candor.

Koe is incredibly brave to bare their soul and reveal their family's story—warts and all—to the world. Like all the best books, *This Heart Holds Many* touches on the deep emotions that connect us all: love, acceptance, togetherness and well-being. Read it! You will be glad you did.

—Dr. Elisabeth Sheff, author of *The Polyamorists Next Door* and *When Someone You Love Is Polyamorous*, and editor of *Stories from the Polycule*

Acknowledgments

At its core, this book is a series of acknowledgments to those involved in my upbringing. In the same way that each relationship has its own unique bond, I would like to speak to a few of the specific ways in which my greater community has supported me in this adventure.

To Snagglepuss: Angi, Gary, Jean, Jim, Phoebe, Royce, Reed and Ember. Without you, this story wouldn't exist. Thank you for being my lighthouse, the place I can navigate from safely and come back to when I need honest perspective. For always calling out my pessimism, listening to my random brainstorms and entertaining my constant performance. There are no others that I would have wished to raise me, or escape from the over-culture with. I love you all deeply.

To Rompas: Lobo, you've seen me all of the way through this process, and it was the kick in the butt you gave me that I needed to get out of my stony haze, put pen to page and bring this vision into reality. I continue to appreciate you challenging me to reach for my goals, no matter how lofty. Te quiero mucho!

To Storm and Tree: Thank you for leaning into the difficult conversations we needed to address in order for me to share this story, with integrity. I've missed you.

To the Sunshine Crew: Rose, Ted, Colin, Jasmine, Deanna, Ben, Bryne et al. The support you have all shown through your genuine inquiry about the authorial process and aid in my domination of Google Docs allowed me to stay present in the process during my most intense moments of writer's block.

You're the community I get to share my twenties with, and I will cherish this time for the rest of my life.

To the Pickle Jar: You are exactly the kind of security I had dreamed of when I was on the journey contained within these pages. I am continuously thrilled to have gotten to sink my roots in and be able to reflect on them enough to share my story with others. It's an honor to get to exercise my newfound skills of adulting and contribute to the sweet, salty brine of the Jar.

To my editors: To Kari Castor, for being my guide. Through your curiosity and insight, you helped me harness the rawness of my vision and craft it into an accessible narrative. Thank you for every answered question and your patience in the face of my procrastination. To Michelle Lingo, for your gentle inquisition and open mind. I hope this story helps the world be a place where your little one can grow up to be exactly who they need to be.

To Thorntree Press: Thank you for providing an avenue for me to share my truth. Your encouragement and guidance through the authorial process is the only reason I will have been able to achieve this goal, which I have been dreaming of for over a decade. You are an inspiration to the polyamorous, sex-positive world, and your willingness to empower multiple voices within it is not unnoticed.

And finally, to all those who have ever been inspired to do something positive for themselves or others based on my presence. You make all of the hard work I do worth it; please keep leaning into your power. We need you.

Glossary

Aunties/uncles: When this reference appears in the text, know that it is how children in my polyamorous community referred to their nonparent adults. During my childhood, nonbinary adults were not presenting to us kids with such terminology, and we never used a nongendered title for an "auntie/uncle" equivalent. As I myself have grown into a nonbinary figure for the next generation of alt-kids, I find myself and my language at a loss for an appropriate term.

BDSM: A culture and philosophy that encourages exploration outside of what is considered "standard" sexual expression. The acronym stands for "Bondage/Discipline, Dominance/submission, Sadism/Masochism." BDSM is also referred to as "kink."

Collectivism: A socioeconomic and cultural system that values groups or communities over individuals. Collectivism is often understood in contrast to individualism, which privileges the individual interests over the group.

Compersion: The feeling of love and joy you have seeing those you love (either your partners or family) experiencing love, joy and success.

Polycule: A metaphor to explain polyamorous relationships using molecular structures and reactions.

Polykid: This term is one I coined to help identify myself as a child growing up in a polyamorous community (similarly to how children of LGBTQ families refer to themselves as "queerspawn"). As we create new additions to language, there will be constant reinvention of terminology. In the 2010s there was an idea brought forth that the use of "poly" in reference to polyamory could be insensitive to those of Polynesian descent who use the term "Poly" to identify themselves as such. With respect to this concept, all references in this book to polyamorous identity have not been shorthanded. The term "polykid" is one that is true for how I referred to myself and my peer group throughout my childhood, and its use is not to supplant or disrespect anyone else's experience. As of 2018, I am working to find a different colloquialism to identify myself with.

Metamour: Another person your partner is in a relationship with, who you are not dating. If B is dating A and C, but A and C are not dating each other, A and C are metamours.

New relationship energy (NRE): The biological hormone cocktail your body mixes up and dumps into your system when you are excited about a new person you'd like to date. Commonly mistaken for long-lasting love. Also what media builds all television romances off of.

Overculture: The dominant culture of modern, mainstream Western society.

Sex positivity: The viewpoint that sex and sexuality are a natural, regular part of one's life; they are not shameful or wrong and can be both celebrated and normalized.

Tribe: A network of people actively engaged in each other's lives. Tribes commonly share resources to mutually support the basic functioning and emotional well-being of those within the tribe.

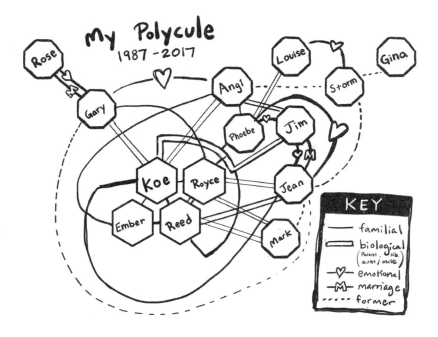

My Polycule
1987-2017

KEY
— familial
▭ biological
(Parent, sib, aunt/uncle)
♡ emotional
M marriage
····· former

Introduction

"Do You Feel Screwed Up Because of Your Childhood?"

In my life, I commonly hear people lamenting the various ways they feel "screwed up" by their childhood, both the experience of inheriting destructive habits from their elders and the need to work through the trauma they incurred in their formative years. "Did your parents screw you up?" is not only a question I have wrestled with internally, but one I have been asked outright when people find out I am the child of sex-positive, polyamorous parents. Instead of getting caught up in lamentation, I have found it more valuable to ask, "How did my parents influence me, and how do I work with that conditioning to create who I want to be?" All five of my parents are the epitome of nerdy, new-agey liberals who date multiple people, are naked more often than clothed and think sex is perfectly natural. All of them have also struggled with poverty, disability, feelings of inadequacy and being misunderstood by the dominant mainstream, which my mother Jean refers to as "the overculture," a culture that has told them they are wrong for being who they are. My parents are flawed, complicated, and also some of the most creative, generous and endlessly communicative people I know.

One of the perks to growing up with five polyamorous, sex-positive parents and a dozen aunties and uncles is that I've seen a multitude of relationships in my life. I have had ample opportunity to witness the whole spectrum of relationships, from disgustingly adorable to downright heartbreaking. Most importantly, though, I have experienced the supportive, caring love of a dozen adults invested in creating a healthy, functioning family for me and my siblings. My childhood was a blessing of infinite love, and the multitude of skills I've learned from my upbringing I now use to aid other prospective parents and polyamorous families to be honest and compassionate with each other while they navigate complex and often misunderstood identities.

If you are a parent or are parent-adjacent, and you are raising a child in the context of your polyamorous lifestyle or navigating how to come out to your child or those in your community about your relationship structure, this book contains numerous anecdotes highlighting the trials, epiphanies and sheer imagination of a polyamorous family creating a successful working dynamic, including their children! Alternatively, if you are someone without children who is looking to gain more understanding about how to support people who are building nonmonogamous families, thanks for taking the time and energy to do so; may you find both insight and tools for how to enact said support with clarity and grace.

What you will find here is not a primer on Polyamory 101; it's a guide on creating and supporting polyamorous families. I assume that, whether you're actively part of the polyamorous community or not, you are familiar with the basic concepts of sex-positivity and nonmonogamy and how they intersect. I encourage you to use this book as a map, outlining some of the landscape for what it realistically takes to create a modern polyamorous tribe and showcasing the mistakes mine made, so hopefully you don't have to. In this book you will find childhood anecdotes, nonchronologically spanning my entire life, highlighting some of my most defining moments as a polykid as well as explanations of the fundamental concepts my family used to raise my siblings and me. Make sure to also keep a look out for the quotes my parents patiently crafted for me during the innumerable out-of-the-blue conversations I started with them during the course of writing this book.

Our parents' influence affects us in a myriad of ways, both positive and negative, but it doesn't mean we are limited by who our parents are or what they taught us. All of my life, I have been asked questions about what my experience was like growing up in a polyamorous family and whether my parents' identities were the reason I turned out as queer, polyamorous and sex-positive as I am. The answer to the latter question is no: I figured it out for myself. Curious about how? I invite you to join me on the adventure contained in the rest of this book. I will tell you all about it!

1
"What Was It Like?"

"I wish there were more polyamorous parents out there that we could have all learned from. Polyamorous families are a generation or two behind LGBTQ families in acceptance and general visibility within society. I also wish you raised-polyamorous kids didn't have to teach polyamory 101 to so many adults." –Jean

Tea Time

The conversation generally starts around the time you are looking to open up to one another about your lives and what brought you to the point you are at now. How you get there changes, but the process of coming out tends to follow the same thread. I talk about my family for half an hour, drawing a silly map in the air in front of me while the person across from me tries to follow my gesticulations while wearing an expression of avid confusion.

Sarah was different, though. She was sweet and intelligent and genuinely laughed at my cheesy gay jokes. It was our second date, and we had been seamlessly chatting for over an hour, barely drinking our tea, just holding our mugs until our hands had drained the warmth from them. I was still figuring out what all I could share with her. She obviously knew I was queer and polyamorous, but I had only hinted at the rest, briefly mentioning my family in passing on our first date. I finally took a deep swig of my cold tea, draining my mug, and set it on the table. When I brought my attention back to her, she was looking at me inquisitively.

The look was familiar, a spark of curiosity laced with apprehension. *Here we go,* I thought. I could tell: Sarah was about to ask the question that all kids who come from heterosexual, happy and monogamous families ask. "If you don't mind me asking, what does your family actually look like? How did that work?" she said in a rush.

I took a deep breath; at least she was curious, and it seemed genuine. I just wished I had a pen and paper on me; it was so much easier to draw. *I should keep a printed copy on me for times like these,* I thought.

Sarah was looking at me expectantly, hoping I would entertain her curiosities. "Like, do you know who your, um—" she paused, and I assumed she was looking for a politically correct way to phrase her question "—b-biological parents are?" she stuttered. I smirked; her apprehension was quite adorable. I was feeling fairly comfortable about having this conversation right now; our location was safe, and I had the patience for it today.

"Yes, I do," I replied plainly. "I have a mom, Angi, a dad, Gary, and I know they are my biological parents. Not all kids of polyamorous families know, though," I added quickly. I needed to make sure she understood it's okay not to know who your bio parents are and that my experience isn't universal to all polyamorous children. "I have some friends who have grown up happily knowing only that they have a bunch of parents taking care of them and loving them all, equally." Sarah nodded, indicating she understood.

"My bio-parents," I went on, "met in the late '80s participating in medieval reenactment through the SCA (Society for

Creative Anachronism). There wasn't a commonly circulated word for nonmonogamy yet; their friend group was just openly promiscuous, and everyone was actively communicating about it. Growing up, they told me about how everyone would all go to the local Denny's, get together and talk about the state of all of their relationships, and how there was a clear sense of tribe among all of them. Some of the members of that tribe started having kids in the early '90s, and several of them decided to raise their kids together, as a unit. That unit is the polycule I consider my family—"

"Polycule?" she interrupted. "What does that mean?"

You have to define it, I thought. "It's like a molecule for your polyamorous life. It's a metaphor that I use to describe how multiple relationships work. I'm a nerd like that." I smiled, and she smiled back brightly. I blushed and continued.

"Anyway, beyond my bio-mom and my bio-dad, I have three other people I consider my polyamorous parents: two other moms and my uncle."

"Your uncle?" she interrupted again. *Geez, she's asking a lot of questions!*

"Yeah, my dad's ex-girlfriend married my mom's brother!" I rattled off. Her brow furrowed, and I giggled. *Got her! Now she'll listen.*

"So, one of my moms, Jean, was dating my bio-dad around the time that my bio-mom and bio-dad met. My dad and Jean's primary partner, Mark, were best friends as well, and my bio-mom met the three of them when she was finding her way into Seattle's alternative community after getting out of the air force. My bio-mom and Jean took a little while to get comfortable with each other, but by the time they were both pregnant (Angi by Gary and Jean by Mark), they had developed a deep friendship; when Jean and my bio-dad broke up, everyone stayed close. Jean's partner Mark left after both of her children were born, and when I was five years old, Jean began dating my Mom's youngest brother, Jim. Jean and Jim got married when I was nine. Jim has always been a close male figure in my life, and he has been very present in my upbringing. I don't consider him a father figure, he's my cool uncle! He's definitely counted as one of my polyamorous parents, though; he's always been there for me."

Sarah let out a soft "Ohhh" of understanding.

"Making sense so far?" I asked. You generally have to check in at this point, to make sure you aren't losing them.

She nodded and then cocked her head. "You said 'both of Jean's children'...how many does she have?" *Wow, she really is paying attention*, I thought. It's always nice when someone catches the details.

"She has two. Royce is my brother. He is four months older than me, and Jean likes to call us 'bookends' for each other. Growing up, we were these opposing forces who, for as much as we butted heads, balanced each other out quite well. Before we started attending school, our parents began teaching us basic academia. Royce was good at math, and I learned to read first. I was a strong, stocky toddler, and he was skinny, nimble and wow, could he run! We were a dynamic duo that raised hell for our parents and taught them the beginning intricacies of navigating kids who were the same age in a blossoming tribal family!" I finished excitedly.

"You've said that a lot, haven't you?" Sarah asked jokingly.

I shrugged nonchalantly. "You know, an interview here, an interview there. You have to have your spiel down for the clamoring media." She outright laughed at me. Little did she know how serious I was; the media had misrepresented my family multiple times, and I had to know how to talk about it. We'd get to that later, if she really wanted to know. I decided to move on.

"And Jean's youngest child is Reed, who is five years younger than Royce and me. Jean and Jim starting dating when Reed was six months old; Reed took to Jim as a father figure over Mark, who is their bio-dad. Jim and Reed are basically two peas in a pod and have been a remarkable example of family being about connection and the investment of time versus straight biology.

I consider Reed to be my closest sibling and best friend in the world. Reed is the person who knows me better than anyone, sometimes including myself. I will bend over backwards for them; using all of my capabilities to help them be successful. At some points this has made me an overbearing big sibling, and Reed has called me on it, stating their own capacity to make mistakes and live their own life—"

Sarah interjected, "Sorry, you keep saying 'them'; how does Reed identify, um, gender-wise?" She was apprehensive again. *Hey, cool, she cares enough to ask.* She didn't want to screw up the gender question. I get it, it's not the easiest to ask for some people, even queer people, and can be important to identify when you are talking about a singular person in a story containing many characters.

"Reed is nonbinary, identifying with male, female, neither, other and sometimes E: all of the above. Reed uses they / them / theirs gender pronouns, and that's how we refer to each other. I also use they / them / theirs pronouns and identify as nonbinary; it's been exceptionally cool to have a common perspective about how to support each other in our gender identity." Her eyes went wide.

Uh-oh, I thought. *Did I take it too far? Was this the aspect of my identity that was just too weird to handle? Maybe I can just wrap up and say goodnight....*

Sarah blurted out, "I am so sorry for misgendering you this whole time!" *Huh, apologies are so rare. Maybe she can actually handle all of my identities.* "I—I mean, you were presenting so femme when we met the other day...I am still getting into the habit of asking anyone, everyone! I mean, it's so important, and I want people to feel safe with me!" I watched her slump a bit then, getting down on herself and making the moment about her inadequacy instead of my gender. *Great, another well-meaning person calling themself an ally without backing it up.* This had become a defining moment: do I pull her up and educate her or just let her sit and not become her personal fountain of knowledge? *Who am I kidding, she's definitely making an effort to act in allyship; so she doesn't have practice with pronouns, at least she knows what they are. Besides, I chose to tell her my life story; I'm already in fountain-of-knowledge mode.*

"It's great that you recognize how asking about people's pronouns is important; I hear your apology and accept it." I dropped my chin and looked over my eyebrows at her. Sarah looked up, frown in full effect.

"Yeah?" she asked.

I held her eye contact and said, "Yeah, we can talk more deeply about my gender later; do you still want to hear the rest about my family? You're doing great; generally people lose interest by this point." I grinned, still holding her eyes. My eye contact is fairly irresistible when I'm feeling confident.

She didn't smile back at me, but she nodded, "Yes, please. I like hearing about your life. I will listen to anything you'd like to share."

"Okay, where was I?" I asked.

"Reed and Royce," she responded without hesitation. *She really is listening*, I reminded myself.

"The third woman I consider to be my mother is a woman named Phoebe, who is Jean's best friend from college and has been in an evolving life partner triad with Jim and Jean since the time I was born. She has no biological children of her own but had almost-daily involvement with Jean's two biological children, Royce and Reed."

She was still staring at me, frowning. I didn't want her to feel like crap; I needed to lighten the mood. "Our parents always told us that Royce and I met when we were in utero. We would get really active; kicking at each other when Angi and Jean were belly to belly. When I was a teenager, the truth came out. One day I was recounting the story I had been told, and Jean candidly shared that this prenatal activity specifically came up when Gary, Angi and she were having a threesome. I was in mild shock, and in classic teenage fashion I needed to confirm this gruesome and disturbing detail of the story. I went directly to Angi, my bio-mom, and accused her of not telling me.

"'Well—' she said, actively failing not to snicker. 'I was waiting for you to grow up a bit before sharing that part with you; but, yes, your dad was having himself a pregnant lady sandwich.'

"I exclaimed, 'Oh my Gods, Mom!' and dropped the conversation while Angi giggled at me, mischievously." Sarah covered her mouth, trying not to choke on her sip of tea. *Yes, I got her to smile!* I went on without pause.

"This was the core family structure throughout my childhood. There were, of course, other tribe members and love interests in my parents' lives. My bio-mom is also the kind of person to 'adopt' all of the local kids and be the cool aunt figure, with everyone calling her the 'Nanny' of the community. There are loads of people to talk about, but these were the people I considered to be my parents and siblings. We've all lived with or near each other throughout my life; my bio-mom and bio-dad ended their romantic partnership when I was about four, and I primarily lived with Angi when I was a kid. Gary did end up living with us again, though, when he was in need of a place to live. My bio-parents have always said that even though they split up romantically, they will always consider each other life partners and co-parents."

I paused to take a breath, and Sarah filled the silence. "Did they get a divorce, though?" she inquired.

"No. They never got married. Their relationship was off-and-on when they had me, so they didn't want to formalize anything they didn't know if they could keep the promise of. The court wasn't there when they made me, why should they be involved in my upbringing? Oh my Gods and Goddesses!" I suddenly clapped my hand to my forehead, very dramatic.

"What is it? Are you okay?" Sarah exclaimed, concerned.

"Yeah, I'm fine. I totally sounded like my dad just now, and it felt so weird!" I began laughing, and I heard her laughing too. Her laugh had such life in it. She had held through the entire explanation and seemed able to roll with it; maybe there was something here that we could build off of.

I took a breath. "Enough about me. What about you? Where did you grow up? What's your relationship with your family like?" I asked animatedly.

Sarah's face became suddenly still and guarded. "Oh, I mean, not nearly as interesting as yours," she said. She looked away from me. *Maybe it's hard for her to talk about it*, I thought.

"You don't have to share if you don't want to, I get it. I also want to let you know, it's not about comparing our families. Just because my childhood takes ten minutes and an infographic to explain doesn't minimize yours. I'd love to hear about you; I will listen to anything that you'd like to share." She visibly relaxed as she looked at me. I winked at her and adjusted myself on the couch, getting into the ideal listening position, ready to hear her share herself with me, whatever that was.

She took a deep breath and began her tale. I listened intently to her life story, making sure to show her the same respect she had shown me. As she shared, I found there to be threads throughout her life that deeply reflected my own experience and helped me ease my feeling of otherness and truly reciprocate the openness she had showed me up until now. Though we came from vastly different backgrounds, our stories weren't entirely different after all.

Adulting, Part One: The Alt-Barbie Princess

I sat there in my aggressively orange-painted ivory tower, amongst the messy pile of blankets and pillows that decorated my gothic four-poster bed. I was staring at my laptop screen through a haze of the newest sativa strain I had spent my last twenty dollars on at the local bud shop. I'd been in this exact situation for over a year, since turning eighteen, with all of the privilege I could've hoped for: a supportive alt-polyamorous family, a stable house in a rich neighborhood, settled in one of the most progressive cities on the North American West Coast. And I was so depressed that I couldn't appreciate any of it.

My fingers sat unmoving on my keyboard while my brain lost itself in endless brainstorms about how I could change the world through sex education and what I should be doing to live up to the hopes and dreams my tribe had for me as their alt-Barbie princess. I was their ideal spokesperson for multigenerational alternative families. I was young, attractive, femme, and a trained actor who loved the spotlight and held all of the same identities and beliefs as my parents and tribe. I had a solid, communicative and loving connection with each of my parents, where not all of the kids in polyamorous families in my generation did. My local tribe subconsciously looked to me to fulfill the relationships they didn't have with their parents or their children, or else they saw me as a role model for their children to look up to and emulate, whether it was natural for them or not. This was solidified for me each time a tribe member asked about what my next project was or did I need any help, and when they expressed their appreciation for me doing the work that I did in the world and being such a good example of a well-adjusted young adult from a polyamorous family.

My tribe wanted success for me so badly that I internalized it. I felt familial pressure that was amplified by how many people it was coming from—an entire community that is always looking for the societal acceptance that the overculture, as my mother calls it, is unwilling to give them. I lived between their pedestal and my own microscope, and I smoked every day to alleviate the pressure. I didn't smoke just to escape, I smoked as a form of self-sabotage. I didn't think I could ever be the projection of what they wanted me to be, so I figured I might as well scramble my brains enough to be unable to accomplish my own goals either. I wanted to move to San Francisco, I wanted to be a famous sex educator who travelled the world, teaching and working for myself, and I wanted to be affluent.

Instead, I found myself stuck living off of my mother's polycule, struggling to get through my days as Seattle's hardest-working second-generation alt-Barbie socialite. I was being who I thought my tribe needed me to be, and what it would take me the next five years to realize is that my tribe didn't need me to be a perfect plastic mold of alternative identity. All they needed was me to be me, believe in myself and do what I needed to be happy. The journey I needed to take to figure that out required me to become the thing I feared the most at the time: a full-fledged adult, an individual who was not merely the byproduct of their upbringing. The story told in the following pages is the one of that journey. From alt-Barbie polykid to self-actualized sex-positive, polyamorous adult and entrepreneur.

In retrospect, I have been able to achieve the kind of success I was yearning for due to the continued support of my tribe, and I would not be the person I am today without them. There is another journey I needed to take, however; I needed to understand the importance of having differing ideologies and opinions than the ones your family holds. I had to move past the trope that says polyamorous families inevitably screw up their offspring, recognizing instead that raising kids in a polyamorous family doesn't actually screw them up any more or less than raising them in any other kind of family. Family is a concept so ubiquitous that I believe no one is excused from thinking about how they relate to it. Whether you feel avoidant of family ties or overwhelmed by them, I believe every person has trauma about their family in one form or another. Not all trauma we receive is a detriment to our lives; instead, sometimes it gives us the resiliency we need to navigate the world. But our trauma does influence how we develop as adults, particularly in our relationships. The goal of understanding your trauma is not to eradicate it, but instead to identify where it came from, what purpose it held in keeping you safe until this point and how it affects your internal landscape now. With this knowledge you can care for yourself and others in a trauma-informed fashion.

When I let my trauma dominate my sense of self-worth, I felt screwed up and I blamed my upbringing, in its entirety. When I was able to begin asking the tough questions, of myself and my family, about the ways in which I felt traumatized, I was able to develop my internal compass for how I was going to need to navigate this life. Through this process of analysis and discovery, I found out which ideologies I agreed with my parents on and which aspects of their worldview I thought were detrimental to achieving my goals. I then not only took the time to let go of these perspectives, but also gave myself time to grieve them; it's not easy to detach yourself from your conditioning when you are looking to maintain a genuine respect for those who conditioned you. I didn't hate my parents, but I did need to feel pity and disappointment towards them for a time. This was a part of seeing them as fully rounded humans versus the two-dimensional parental archetypes they had previously been to me.

Once I was able to reconcile these shadows and focus on how to move forward as an individual, the positive qualities of my upbringing, such as generosity, honesty and empathy, began to flourish and I was able to harness them, catapulting myself towards the goals I had only dreamt about in the stony haze of my teenage bedroom. Understanding how your family influenced your thinking is a process that naturally happens as one grows up, but I do not believe we are taught that as individuals we are the ones who can take active control over this process. I have seen multiple second-generation children of polyamorous families become more and more resentful of their parents and their upbringing as they reach adulthood and never develop the vulnerable, supportive and healthy relationship I have with my family today.

The kind of parental support I have is a privilege I wish more people had access to. I hope this book, which outlines my personal experiences being raised in a sex-positive, polyamorous family, shows people how parents and children can mutually support each other in navigating the murky waters of identity exploration and relationships.

2

"Who Are Your Real Parents?"

"One of the strengths of having a polyamorous family is that it creates a village that spans the world, where physical proximity isn't the joining factor, but a commitment to each other and their significant others."–Jean

Collectivist Culture

I was impatient with excitement. Angi, Gary and Jean had all come to the first parent-teacher meeting that I was also there for, and they had brought along baby Shae, the toddler of one of Gary's lovers who had recently moved in with us. I sat there, beaming, my adolescent attention focused on how amazing it was to have my family come visit me at school, blissfully unaware of the awkward tension the conversation was stewing in. My fourth-grade teacher, Barbara, was obviously boggled by the amount of people staring back at her from the other side of the table. She was tripping over her words, and her eyes kept darting between the three parents and fussy toddler as she tried to describe my academic performance throughout the first half of the year.

Looking back, I recognize it must not have been easy for my elementary school teachers to figure out exactly how my family operated. We were a complex web of various adults and children who were rarely all in the same place at the same time and expected the people we had regular interactions with to keep up. Unlike other nonnuclear family structures, such as children raised with the help of a grandparent or older sibling, in polyamorous families it is not always obvious how people are connected to the child or who the primary guardians are. Without asking directly, which could be construed as impolite, how is an educator supposed to know who to direct their questions to?

My schoolteacher's struggles in communicating with us were probably made worse by the fact that my family is very bold and detail oriented in our communication style. Each member of my family has their own flavor of exuberance, and we are inquisitive, occasionally argumentative and highly intelligent. Having so many cooks in the proverbial kitchen, collaborative coordination was crucial to our daily successes, and we would not disengage from a topic until we had all of the pertinent information we needed to move forward.

When it came to us kids' public education, our parents tried to be forthcoming with our operating procedure, but there's only so much the structure of the public-school system was able to provide us. Mine was an alternative education public school started in early-1990s Seattle, a far more open and liberal situation than it could have been. We were dealing with a less than hostile circumstance, and yet there was no awareness or support structure for nonmonogamous families in public education. Ellen DeGeneres had only just come out as gay, and the US was barely beginning to understand that the visibility of nonheteronormative people was only going to get stronger after the height of the AIDS epidemic.

My teacher was dealing with a structure for which there was no context and with a family who was constantly asking a barrage of questions, trying to get five parents' worth of concerns addressed—no wonder she was overwhelmed! We knew she was trying her best to work within the framework she was given.

Barbara was visibly nervous as she brought up the next topic. "I understand that you all take care of Koe and would like to be kept informed. I just don't think I can have more than two people down as emergency contacts or be able to pick Koe up from school, unless they are a direct relative. It's a safety issue—"

Jean cut her off by explaining, "Seattle Public Schools allows babysitters to pick up children from schools, whether they are relatives or not. Besides, we *are* Koe's direct relatives." Being a child of a neo-Pagan hippie family herself, Jean always had the creative workarounds for bureaucratic situations like this. "Gary and Angi are Koe's parents. Jim is Koe's uncle and I am his wife, Koe's aunt. Phoebe is our babysitter; this should all fit within your definition of allowable."

She took a deep breath to keep going before anyone else could cut in, but Gary and Angi just sat back and let her go. When Jean got on a roll, stopping her was a Herculean task that Angi and Gary knew better than to undertake. "As far as being a safety concern, how is it safer to have fewer people to call in case of an emergency? Angi and Gary both work on the other side of the water and would be stuck in forty-five minutes of traffic, minimum, to get here. Whereas I regularly have house-cleaning clients in this area and could be here in fifteen minutes. Now, who would you prefer dealing with: a parent who has spent the last hour frustratedly trying to get to their sick or injured child? Or someone who could easily pop by and pick up the sick or injured kiddo?" Jean chuckled and that gave the self-satisfied smile she wore whenever she knew she had out-logicked an authority figure.

My teacher raised a bewildered eyebrow and said, "How about we just attach another page to the form and you can put all of the people you need to."

Angi took over and said, "Thank you, we will."

My parents came together each with their own background in collectivism, from Angi's extended family of Midwestern farmers to Jean's childhood upbringing on a commune in the Willamette Valley; each drew on their personal experiences with collective living to build a support network for themselves and their children. As a family, we found solace in any sentiment that reflected to us that our decisions were not wrong, and that we were not unique in executing them. My mothers quoted examples of the alternative family structures depicted in Robert Heinlein's works often enough that by ten years old, I could quote segments from *The Moon is a Harsh Mistress* even though I had never read the book.

Later, in my teenagehood, the book *Sex at Dawn* came out and corroborated many of the ideas about collectivist culture that had influenced how my parents operated in their nonmonogamy. In *Sex at Dawn* Christopher Ryan and Cacilda Jethá highlight research done on the nature of humanity before the advent of agriculture and thus the idea of a legacy to protect. This was a time of hunter-gatherer tribes living collectively, pooling their resources and looking out for their own. After the advent of agriculture, the perception shifted towards humans having the right to own parcels of the earth to steward and pass on to their kin. This perception meant biological connection was of the utmost importance, as one needed to know where their genes were going so they had someone to pass on the inheritance to. Over generations, this focus on biology birthed the idea of the nuclear family and fed into the larger concept of individualism, in conjunction with patriarchal capitalism, as the dominant narrative. Due to this intentional re-focusing, collectivism was then marginalized and has been given less credence when discussed as applicable for modern-day use. Despite this intentional erasure, however, collectivist culture has continued to have many iterations throughout history and exists among large families and communities throughout the world today.

As the colonialist dominance of patriarchal Western culture took hold in North America, there was a focused propagation of individualism as people's ideal state of being. Phrases such as "every man for himself" have built a society that has cut off the lines of empathy for fellow humans and replaced them with distrust for otherness, which feeds directly into the narratives around how to love, and how to build family. The most common narrative states, "Find your one true match, get married, have children, live in your own home and be happy until you die." With the divorce rate at around fifty percent for married couples in the US, it seems that this narrative may be a bit narrow for the society it's advertising to.

Though my parents and the community they associated with in their young adulthood were a group of people who came from different ancestries and upbringings, their interactions were based on the ideas of mutual support and creative collaboration. One of the common threads that brought them together was the feeling of otherness, of feeling antithetical to the values of the society they were currently living in. This was a society built out of imperialism that placed importance on values such as individualism and proprietary ownership, values that naturally breed monogamy. I have always found it ironic that the societal teachings touted as "traditional" are actually more nouveau than the "hippie" ideals my family was teaching me. I have had to reconcile that many pieces of my family's ideology were appropriated from other cultures; but I also understand that though my family was cherry-picking the aspects of world culture that supported their personal philosophy, they were doing so to try to create a well-rounded, humanist container in which to live in a modern tribe.

As a child born into that tribe, I had the privilege of having multiple people whom I knew I could trust and lean on for support of all forms. Everything from learning a basic skill to being able to choose whom I processed my deepest fears with was available to me. My parents were a wealth of resources on their own, and in combination with the extended tribe I have never felt alone or unsupported in my dreams. There were absolutely frustrations with having that many adults all up in your business; the mornings where I had multiple parents ask me whether I'd finished unloading the dishwasher before I'd even made it to the breakfast table were particularly annoying. But as I have grown up, I have been overcome with gratitude for the way each of the adults in my tribe chose to have a vested interest in my life.

Mine is also one perspective within a mosaic of experience. The loving and mutually respectful parent-child relationship is not true for all children of polyamorous families, nor is it even the same experience other children were having within my tribe. By nature, humans experience situations differently, and it is important to consider this when engaging with a second-generation polyamorous person. You know how annoying it is when someone assumes you had a positive experience when the opposite is true? Imagine that concept applied to your entire childhood. When they are not having to defend their familial structure, children of polyamorous families are often exotified by people who are trying to be supportive.

The statement "Wow, that must've been so great for you!" is common, and it is also a gross oversimplification of a complex experience. When you come into contact with a child of a polyamorous family, my suggestion is to thank the person for sharing this piece of information and inquire if you may ask a few questions about their experience, only after you have had several paragraphs of conversation with them, learning about them as an individual. If they agree to answer your questions, please make your first one be "What was it like for you?" Allow them the opportunity to share their truth instead of clarifying the narrative you have undoubtedly built in your head about their upbringing.

Many of the negative experiences that kids I grew up with have spoken to come from their dynamics with their parents, on the whole. Polyamory played a role occasionally, but the tension still consistently seems to have centered on how the adults acted throughout situations versus the concept of nonmonogamy itself. This is also not inherently true for all children of polyamorous families; some have ethical or moral disagreements with their parents' ideology, and these children's perspectives are also valid (the idea of validity is discussed more fully later in this chapter). It is important to remember that each person, though influenced by their upbringing, is not fully defined by it.

I met Sue as a teenager. We had both grown up in the greater alt-Seattle community, with polyamorous parents, and I had known her vaguely since I was young. We began to get closer when her family started coming to my Pagan church with regularity, and we naturally gravitated towards each other, being in the same age bracket. As the months passed, I was becoming increasingly smitten and wanted nothing more than to have her as my primary girlfriend. She held care for me but was an emotionally reclusive type and would rarely bring herself to acknowledge our relationship publicly, though we spent the majority of our time together, going on dates frequently, and got "married" at a Renaissance faire. Here's to young love, the endearing series of chaotic misadventures that shape us forever! She was the daughter of a polyamorous lesbian and did not have a good relationship with her mom for a variety of reasons. Sue identified as polyamorous and bisexual herself but was adamant that it had nothing to do with her mother's influence.

Among many things Sue introduced me to, the one that would come to change my life was Camp Ten Trees, a summer camp created specifically for LGBTQ teens and children of LGBTQ families. I had heard her go on and on about the camp, and I was determined to experience it for myself. The first year I went (I was fifteen), she and I were assigned to the same cabin, and throughout the week she continued to chuckle at me and my excited delirium about it all. I felt like I was living in a dream, an incredibly gay dream I hadn't known I had been fantasizing about all of my life. I never went to summer camp as a kid and didn't have any context for how this summer camp was different from that experience, but I knew that I was surrounded by a higher concentration of specifically LGBTQ people than ever before. In addition to having a dozen new crushes on various campers and being in total awe of the counselors, I could look up to and see myself in...everyone. At camp, people seemed to be fully present in their identity and were showing themselves off, with pride. I admit, I was in a fairly constant state of wide-eyed compersion and took every possible opportunity to thank Sue for showing me this magical place.

Inside of our cabin, it was known that she and I were dating, which was against the rules of the summer camp, but we had omitted that particular detail on our applications so we could be in a cabin together. We weren't in trouble, but we had to give our counselors our word that we wouldn't break any camp rules by acting overtly sexual or exhibiting exclusive behavior. We gave our promise. We weren't in the kind of relationship where we needed to be all over one another, and I was developing such a deep love of the camp that I wouldn't have even considered breaking the rules for fear of being unable to come back. The other members of our cabin were powerful, gregarious femmes who held a wealth of sexual experience and enjoyed talking about sex, sexuality and relationships at every opportunity.

After we had collectively grilled our counselors for every juicy detail they would give us about their lives, we began trading stories, preferences and anecdotes with each other about our experiences. Being the insatiable pervert I have always been, I was invested in the conversation and milking every sexual experience I'd had for all it was worth, making myself out to be a sixteen-year-old queer Casanova. Each time I would look at Sue during these conversations, she would blatantly roll her eyes at me.

Eventually our other cabinmates caught on to the fact that I was talking about multiple people in addition to Sue, and they turned to her to see how she felt about these claims. They asked her if she was mad about me fooling around with all of these other people, and she said, "It's fine by me, I know Koe isn't doing anything dangerous, and we are polyamorous after all." The conversation stalled, the air got thick, and I felt the question coming before it filled the cabin.

"Poly-what?" they asked.

"Polyamorous. It means we also have other partners in addition to each other, and everyone knows and is okay with it," Sue said plainly. I looked at her with adoration. She truly knew how to succinctly shut people up with her no-bullshit attitude.

I looked back to our cabinmates, who were staring at us, obviously formulating a million more questions. In this moment, I recognized they hadn't heard of polyamory before, and it was a bit astonishing to me. I had assumed that being in an LGBTQ space meant that people must obviously know about polyamory, but by the looks on their faces, it seemed clear that this was not true. After they asked us a bunch of questions about our relationship and our other partners—and after a check-in from our counselor about whether Sue and I were comfortable answering all of these questions—the subject of our parents came up. "Do your parents know? How do they feel about it?"

Sue and I immediately looked at each other and burst into giggles. Our cabinmates jumped at our reaction and one of them asked, "What's so funny?"

When Sue and I regained out breath, she said, "They don't mind at all, as they are polyamorous themselves!" I stared at Sue, her smug face relishing the other campers' wide-eyed surprise. I couldn't help it; it was a big deal.

She rarely ever brought up her mom in public and admitted so readily that she was second-generation polyamorous. When I would question her on this, she generally expressed to me that she didn't feel it was most people's business. In my mind, this was the magic of summer camp at work, and I would wholeheartedly support her through this conversation as long as she wanted it to last. The natural follow-up question came from our cabinmates, and I was ready for it.

"Are you polyamorous because your parents are?" someone asked.

I responded briskly, "Are you queer because your parents are?" My response had come out snarkier than I had intended, but it seemed to be the right level of blunt for my cabinmates, as thoughtfulness spread across their faces. I followed up with, "What I mean is, just because your parents do something doesn't mean you have to. We might have learned about polyamory sooner than others, but I know I chose this for myself."

I looked to Sue for a confirmation that this was also true for her, and she shrugged, responding, "Basically."

The conversation continued from there, our cabinmates asking us thoughtful questions for the next hour until we had to head to the dining hall for dinner. Upon leaving the cabin, I walked with Sue a little behind the rest and asked her how she was doing. "Fine, why?" she responded, neutralizing any emotional reaction she was having to the situation because we were in public.

Understanding that the general nature of summer camp meant we were never going to get the chance to truly be alone, I knew I needed to check in right then, before the moment passed, so I said, "Because I've never heard you defend your mom and her partner like that before."

She stopped on the boardwalk and turned to me. "Just because my mom isn't great at relationships doesn't mean I don't believe in what she and her partners are doing. Polyamory works for me right now and I can share knowledge with people who are curious about it, so why wouldn't I?" I gulped hard and nodded, daring myself not to tell her how much I loved her, because I knew it would make her uncomfortable. Recognizing this, she rolled her eyes at me again, grabbed my hand and said, "Come on, we have to catch up. They'll think we're making out, and then we'll be in real trouble."

I learned a lot about Sue through that conversation, and though she continued to rarely show her emotionality in regard to her relationships, familial or romantic, I knew Sue held a certain sense of compassion and understanding for the polyamorous part of her upbringing, no matter what her relationship with her mom was.

It's no secret that relationships take work, so when you are engaging in multiple relationships that you care about equally, that work naturally multiplies. When you are engaging in those relationships within the context of a tribe, the amount of consciousness you need to bring to the work you are doing means the variables for entropy increase. Polyamorous relationships have infinite capacity to hurt as much as their capacity is to create loving joy, and this fact is often used to try and discredit polyamory as a legitimate relationship style. If you are looking to be supportive when engaging with children of polyamorous families, which I hope you are, it is important to acknowledge this rhetoric without attaching judgment to it. My mothers have always loved to use the phrase "It takes a village to raise a child." But there have never been guarantees that members within the proverbial village won't make mistakes along the way. Hopefully, the children are able to have a bevy of mentors to learn responsible integrity from and are not bound to the sole example of their biological parents. This is the strength I believe Christopher Ryan and Cacilda Jethá speak to in *Sex at Dawn* when talking about the value of highly connected groups such as hunter-gatherer tribes.

Ergonomic Relationships

It was a sweltering summer day in my turn-of-the-century studio apartment. What the little place lacked in climate control it made up for in charm; I was immensely proud of my first home outside of my parents' houses and took every opportunity to show it off. On this afternoon, Jim had come over to share a bowl and talk about the various issues going on in our lives. The tradition began in my late teens when I became old enough to start smoking marijuana.

After we had exhausted all of our various grievances with the other members of our family, I felt a question bubble up in me that I had never asked before. I gave Jim a significant enough look that he stopped mid-toke and choked on the smoke. I laughed at him, then apologized as he began hacking up a lung.

Once he recovered and called me a brat, he asked me, "So, did you have something you wanted to say, Miss Drama Queen?"

Blushing, I asked him, "Did you actually end up adopting Reed and Royce?"

He looked down at his pipe and fiddled with the ashes inside the bowl. Jim isn't the best at eye contact when he's nervous. "No, I wasn't able to because Mark never gave up his parental rights. I would have, in a heartbeat, a fucking New York minute, someone just had to show me where to sign the dotted line and it would've been done!" he said.

I cocked my head in curiosity. "Was that for emotional or legal reasons? Mark not giving up his rights—"

Jim responded before I could finish my sentence. "Legal. Emotional connection wasn't the question. They were my kids, especially Reed, since Mark left the picture when they were so young."

"That's right, Reed was three years old, I remember." I said.

Jim nodded and continued, "Having a formal adoption could've made things easier if it was ever legally necessary. Thankfully, we never encountered a situation that required it, and Mark stayed away from the family, so it all worked out in the end." Jim shrugged and with a small grimace ritualistically reached for his plastic baggie to fill another bowl. The action itself wasn't out of the ordinary, but his reaching for more medicine so reflexively after sharing his thoughts with me told me that the topic still ate at him on some level. I let it be, though, let him have his feelings without trying to analyze them. For better or worse, Jim had raised Reed and Royce as their father, and for better or worse, they considered him as such. The legality was just another layer of complication that made explaining our family difficult to do without pen and paper.

I know I have always hated the question "Who was your real parent growing up?" Aside from being ignorant, it has always been difficult to answer because of its basis in a totalitarian way of thinking about relationships. My family did not work well with totalitarianism but instead functioned through ergonomic relating. Being the nerds we are, we used this applied science concerned with designing and arranging people and things to interact most efficiently and safely, and we applied it to how we built our relationships.

Let's do a thought experiment: you walk into a children's toy store and are looking around. Your attention is pulled towards a popular doll. In familiar fashion, the doll is fully equipped with outfits, accessories and a backstory; it's all ready for you to pull out and play with. As you are scanning the rest of the aisle, you see a jumbo bucket of multicolored building blocks! All of the blocks are different shapes and serve different functions but are equally compatible with all of the other blocks in the bucket. They come with a handy booklet that's filled with ideas of what you could build with the blocks but does not restrict your play by assuming what you are going to build with them. Seeing both of these options and knowing you can only bring home one of the toys, which do you choose?

There is no wrong answer in this experiment; each person is going to relate to the toys differently. My family happened to choose the building blocks as their preferred toy. The decision of how you could relate was also extended to my siblings and me. We had functional autonomy over the ways each of our relationships functioned with our nonbiological parents and their partners. If I didn't like someone one of my parents was dating, the approach was the same as when trying out a new food: I was asked to try interacting with them to see if spending more time together helped me change my perspective. If we clearly didn't get along, I was never forced to take direction from them and was allowed to keep them at a distance. In contrast, if there was a partner whom I developed a deep connection with, and the relationship they were having with my parent ended, my parent would offer me the opportunity to continue my interaction with the former partner. This was, of course, always offered within the context of my parents agreeing that the former partner in question was a healthy enough human to safely continue a friendship with their child.

My bio-parents specifically worked at not burning bridges with their former partners so they would be able to assist me in maintaining that connection. I have no doubt it was difficult for them, but it simultaneously encouraged them to foster healthier tribal dynamics by breaking up harmoniously within their insular community. The ability to maintain such relationships led me to be able to develop the kinds of adult mentorships that could provide me advice, guidance and support from outside of my parents' direct sphere of influence. Through maintaining these connections, not only have I been able to get the different perspectives I needed to develop my personal sense of identity, but I have also been able to help these elders in different ways, like helping them figure out their own kink identity and providing witness to their marriage ceremony. I would not have been able to do these things if my parents had restricted how I got to interact with these humans.

I have developed this building block metaphor after seeing thousands of relationships develop that did not follow a generic script that was handed to them by the overculture. Even when it was an internally focused dyad (like a closed couple), I saw people take the time and effort to think critically about what they were building; they agreed on what they were mutually interested in and consciously chose which aspects of the relationship they wanted to use to accomplish their goals.

Every relationship is a set of people playing with building blocks in the way that works best for them! Even if at some point in the relationship you need to restructure the sculpture you have been building for years, perhaps taking out a fundamental color of building block (an aspect of the relationship), and build something new, it doesn't mean that you've broken your toy. You now get the chance to build something else that will work, if differently than before. I also enjoy this metaphor because when you both are done playing with your building blocks, you can take everything apart, putting away all of your blocks without having lost the capacity to build with them again. This way of thinking gives you access to use these foundational pieces, saving them for use later if you all find there's continued interest in playing together.

Yes, there are also times when you are not having fun playing with this person anymore, and you end up knocking over the sculpture, scattering pieces across the floor and not bothering to clean up the mess. In these cases I strongly encourage you to focus on the following questions, which will help you frame the relationship in the larger context of your life and, hopefully, breed out the resentment that can build post-relationship:

- What did you learn from this game?
- Which blocks did you most enjoy using?
- Could you have been more specific about the kind of play you want?
- Did you leave yourself open to new kinds of play you hadn't considered before?
- Are there new strategies you learned that you would like to play with in the future?

Now that we have a working understanding of the concept of ergonomic relating, I get to truly blow your mind. This concept applies to families as much as partners and friends. Boom! Okay, you might have seen that coming, but I do find that this is the place where I start to get the most pushback from people when explaining this concept. I often hear something like "You can't choose your family, children have their parents and they have to listen to them." Which I generally respond to with a significant eye roll.

News flash: chosen family exists all over the place, and ergonomic relating is a fabulous dynamic not just for creating healthy nonmonogamous connections and close-knit friend groups. The ergonomic focus is also essential to building successful nonbiological family connections. Let's say a parent with a partner they have been seeing for a while is ready to introduce the partner to the child. Here are some natural questions that come up for the partner:

- How does the parent want me to act with the child?
- What role am I going to take in this child's life?
- How do I connect to this child so that they like me?
- Will the child even have an interest in having me around?

Through my work, I have discussed these questions with dozens of nonbiological parents and understood the concept from the child's perspective. More recently I have found the same curious concerns ringing true for myself, as my generation is getting older and I am beginning to date people who have children, who I will get the privilege to develop connections with.

Just like with the development of romantic relationships, each relationship the child develops with the adults in their life is going to look different. My relationship with each of my mothers is based on love, mutual caring and the need for guidance, but the manifestation of that dynamic looks different based on the people and how we decided, through both our actions and intentional conversations, to build them.

My mother Phoebe is the only mother to not have given birth to any of us kids and is the only one of my parents I haven't lived with. Neither of these dynamics makes her any less of a mother to me. This small amount of differential experience has provided value for me throughout my life; she has been the primary person I have gone to for outside perspective on issues going on at home with my siblings and other parents. She is the one who taught me how to tie my shoes, brush my hair and take a time-out when I need it, so I don't escalate myself to the point of an overstimulated meltdown. She has held me through hardship and praised me for my accomplishments. I always knew I could count on her to be present in my life when I needed her, and knew she had full right to punish me when I had done wrong. Phoebe intentionally made the decision when Royce and I were gestating about whether she wanted to be an ongoing part of the family we were creating. She and my parents discussed in what capacity she wanted to be involved in our everyday upbringing and what being a mother meant to her. Though as much conversation as they had, she has still told me, "No matter how much talking we did, there was no way to tell what your true impact on me would be until you were born and I was living it. You gave me the blessing of getting to experience being a mother in the ways I could handle." I could not imagine my life without Momma Phoebe in it, and luckily I don't have to.

Phoebe is a good example of an established ergonomic relationship, but sometimes the relationships that end up developing are the ones you least expect. Ember was an intelligent, spritely young human who bounced their way into our family purely of their own volition. When Ember was ten, their biological family began attending the weekly polyamorous potlucks held at the huge polyamorous house my mother and I lived in through my later teenage years. Initially, I felt a competition with Ember due to our similar personalities and the uncanny physical resemblance we shared. But Ember and Angi started developing a deep connection right away, and I had the sense that no matter how I felt, Ember was somehow going to be a part of our family. Ember figured out that though Angi was the "Nanny" to all of the tribe, there was still a subset of people she saved a particular kind of nurturing for. These were not just her kiddos, but her children.

Ember saw this and immediately knew they wanted to be a part of Angi's inner circle. Ember approached Angi one day and asked, "Nanny, how do I get adopted by you?"

Angi responded, "My dear, you already have been. You are a beloved part of this tribe."

Ember shook their head and said, "No, I mean how do I become one of your children, like Reed and Royce are?" Angi's eyes apparently became the size of dinner plates at this point. She had never experienced someone pursue her for adoption in this way; she had either raised the child since birth or had slowly developed a rapport with the person and eventually informed them that she would like to consider them as her child in the tribe.

Angi needed a few things cleared up before saying yes flat out. She started by laying out her capacity and hard limits. "Now, Ember. I want to make sure you know what you are asking for. When it comes to all of my children, just like Koe as my bio-kid, you will always be able to call me and ask for advice, and you will always have a person to call in the middle of the night if you need to be rescued, without questions or judgment. You are welcome at all of our family gatherings, but as my kid you will be able to come over to the house any time you want, and you and I can do creative projects together. I want to make it clear, though: I cannot take the place of your biological mother. You won't be able to live with me full time, and I won't be adopting you legally."

Ember nodded approvingly. "I know, Nanny. I love my mom and don't expect to you to take over for her. I want an adult I can talk to and do the special things I see you and your other kids do. Not just the fun stuff; also the work parties and being Nanny's helper. I want it all, and I want that with you!" Angi tried to blink the tears from her eyes. She was so moved by the clarity and eloquence with which this preteen was able to express what they were interested in. Ember wanted to develop the kind of connection that goes beyond that of an auntie, someone you can have deep respect and care for; they were truly asking for a Momma in their life. With a Momma, the child will always know they have a safety net both physically and emotionally from that person; the child is able to form a bond of emotional intimacy that will be unshakeable. From the Momma's perspective, the child will be one of the ones the Momma gives distinct time and attention to and holds responsibility for. The Momma is the one that you let the deepest into your heart space and hold the highest respect for.

Amid her musing, Angi's rationality kicked in once again, and she realized she hadn't responded in a few minutes. She came back to herself and responded to Ember, "Well, okay then. It sounds like you've thought about this quite a bit. I would be happy to try it out and see how we feel in a couple of months."

Ember lit up like buzzing firefly. "Okay, Nanny, that sounds great!" at which point Ember flung themself into Angi's arms and they shared a deep, squishy hug.

When they broke apart, Angi gave Ember a serious look. "You know this also means you will be considered a Minion and will be given duties as such. You will be expected to give back to the tribe—"

Ember cut Angi off, reassuring her, "I know, Nanny. Reed already told me all about being a Minion and that it would be great to have help so they weren't the only one now that Royce and Koe are older and don't do as much Minioning anymore." (Minion: the helpful role children take on in the tribe. See "Adult on Deck" in Chapter Three for details.) Nanny knew this was something she couldn't argue with and therefore just nodded her assent. They hugged again and returned to the rest of us having potluck, beaming like they'd each just received a brand-new kitten for their birthday.

Angi and Ember's maternal relationship blossomed steadily over the next year. Ember began coming over for "Nanny sleepovers" and attending all of our family events. Ember had spoken with their family about the newfound connection and seemed to be negotiating it well. Reed had fully accepted having a sibling closer to their age and was thrilled to not take on the brunt of Minioning duties the tribe was asking of them. I, however, continued to keep my distance.

When it came to new adopted siblings, I was generally a bit of a holdout, and it only got more intense the older I became. Even being raised within a huge polyamorous tribe, throughout most of my daily life it was just Angi and me; biologically I am an only child, and my tendencies lean towards territorial protection of my relationship with my mother. Through thick and thin, Angi and I were each other's primary emotional counterpart, and I would not let anyone get in the way of that.

My attachment to my intense emotional dynamic with Angi was deeply fed by Angi's decision to refocus her life on me through later parts of my primary development. When I was eight years old, Angi saw that I was having a difficult time dealing with her and Gary breaking up with people and not having access to them anymore when I had spent energy building relationships with them. All of my parents agreed that when a relationship ended, the children would have the choice to continue safely engaging with the former partner in question. In addition to the parents making this intentional decision about how to reframe their breakups, Angi also decided to become celibate for a time, which included no dating. She did this so that I could have a stable parent to connect with when the loss of other parents' partners was too much for my adolescent self to deal with. Her celibacy ended up lasting for seven years, as I grew from a child into a rip-roaring teenager! Around my fifteenth birthday, she began dating again, and I reacted like a cat who had just been given their first bath. I felt threatened, violated, and I wanted to rage, which I was expressing as passive-aggressive indifference towards anyone new in her life. It did not matter whether the person was a lover or an adoptee into her own personal pack of polykids.

Over the next year, I ended up calming down after several impressive rows with Angi where I was quickly taught what slut-shaming was and was forced to deal with the consequences of perpetuating it towards Angi. I realized that I was lashing out because I was afraid of losing my connection with my biological mother and being replaced by a partner. Once I was finally able to express this, Angi was able to reassure me that no matter how many partners or nonbiological children she had in her tribe, there would only ever be one person she grew in her body and raised by her side: "Nothing in this world could ever replace you, pumpkin."

By the time we had come to live with the quad Angi had settled with, I was sixteen and had become comfortable with the idea of my mom dating again. Angi was less focused on being promiscuous and was leaning into building deeper connection with her current serious partners. She and I had also discussed the parameters of my interest in engaging with her various new sweeties and that I would need some extra time and space for anybody new she wanted to bring into our mutual life. She agreed to this, then proceeded to "adopt" three new children, including Ember, in the span of nine months. This was one of those moments where I learned the need to be exceptionally specific with my words when negotiating my needs. Angi was in a huge time of expansion and building community at this time;

she was perfectly in her right to connect with new children, and I hadn't said I had a problem with that in any way.

By the time I found my words and was able to express my needs to Angi, she had already solidified her connection with these new "siblings," including Ember. I needed time and space to figure out what I, as the biological child, was going to be with these people. To her credit, once I had spoken my needs to Angi, she was in total support of me doing what I needed to do for myself and was impeccable about making sure I continued to feel special in our connection as biological mother and daughter, reassuring me that nothing and no one would change that.

There was also something specific about Ember that caused me a deep discomfort. Ember was energetic, fantasy oriented, performative, a model and an aspiring actor. Ember also happened to have my same hairstyle, and we looked more alike than any of my other siblings. I was having a hard time not feeling like they were my Mini-Me and my mom was trading me in for a younger model. It was Reed, using their wonderfully blunt capacity to cut through bullshit, who said, "You're being really egoistic and self-centered about this. Ember's a great person who is different from you and you actually have a lot to learn from them." Even when younger siblings are cutting with their words, I have found they generally hit the nail on the head about you living in your negativity.

Eventually, I opened myself to Ember and discovered a delightfully curious human who was defining themselves not by their parents and circumstance, but through intentional inquisition and carefully choosing what they wanted to explore before they decided to engage. As our relationship continued to deepen, Ember and I found more and more ways in which we were alike but just different enough that we were able to show each other a different perspective on the same topic for mutual benefit. Though Ember agreed that they also felt a certain kinship in being my Mini-Me, I have let go of that comparison and now simply beam in awe of who they are becoming, especially in all of the realms I didn't get to follow through on. That's one of the joys of being an older sibling, I've found: getting to help younger siblings recognize their deepest desires and witness them live out their dreams, struggles and all. For a biologically only child, I consider this a true blessing I would not have gotten to participate in if not for ergonomic relationships.

Think about a significant relationship you have had; it could be a lover or friend, someone you mutually chose to engage with. Think about when you first connected with this person:

- Did you enjoy their presence right away?
- How long did it take to become comfortable with one another and start letting your walls down?
- What kind of dynamic do you find yourselves in now?

Take a minute, lean into these thoughts, and refer back to them as you consider these next questions:

- How did your dynamic come to be this way?
- Did you converse about your desires and capacity before formalizing the relationship?
- If the relationship came about organically, how did you know what you were open to engaging in?

I encourage you to think of your relationships less as a package deal that you buy and try to make fit your interests and desires. Instead, I'm offering a style of relating that is like a series of pieces you get to play with to create what works for the both, or all, of you at the time. You are always allowed to revisit your game and renegotiate both your structural design and the blocks you want to use to build it. Remember, this your life to live exactly the way you need to; why not make the most of it?

Validity

Living your life exactly as you need to is an important concept to get comfortable with, within yourself, and try to live out as boldly as you can! I have also found this to be an infinitely more challenging task without some form of external validation for your boldness. It doesn't help that validity, outside of the context of hard sciences, is a fairly nebulous concept. What truly constitutes something being "valid"?

In general, you should not need to present your identity to be judged as "worthy enough" to engage in community; this is a job for your accountability and integrity of action. Your internal identity is valid, and that can be enough. The primary goal of this chapter is to highlight how positive reinforcement of someone's thoughts and identity through validation can drastically affect their internal experience and sometimes their quality of life.

I have experienced this as a concept starting from within but generally needing confirmation from outside sources to be accepted as consensus reality. My reality growing up was this: kids had many parents and mentors who all came together to create community and raise children. Some of them dated one another at different times, but it made them no less of a functioning tribe member if they were not dating anyone in the tribe. This perspective specifically de-emphasizes the power given to couples and heredity, instead focusing on the concept my mother(s) always described as "effort and attitude," meaning how much effort did you put into the task at hand, and what was your attitude in doing so? If someone was vetted as an ethical human with similar morals who continued to show up and provide value to the tribe, they were welcomed. If their actions began to show the tribe they were unable to keep to their word or their intentions were incongruous with that of the tribe, it was then that they either distanced themself or were asked to leave.

The Western dominant culture of the twentieth century did not teach this ideology when it came to love, relationships or building families. Throughout my life, when explaining this concept—which appears to me as no less valid than any other family structure—to those of the overculture, I have found myself spouting lengthy exposition and receiving opinions or advice that I did not ask for. It has been rare that I divulge the relatively simple statement "I have three moms" and said statement is taken at face value and accepted. I understand that it is human nature to question things that are not understood to gain clarity, but without conscientiousness this line of inquiry easily leads to someone else questioning the validity of my reality. When your reality is consistently questioned, it breeds an insecurity about whether you and your beliefs are able to be trusted and if there is something "wrong" with you. Uninterrupted, this insecurity can develop into issues with shame and depression. The overculture continuously perpetuates ideals, and when anyone deviates from them, they are demoted into being a social minority wrought with stereotyping and oppressive messaging deeming them as "lesser," feeding into the aforementioned insecurity and perpetuating the cycle of depression. Therefore, it is crucial as we develop our relationships with our loved ones to practice compassion and trust of people when they are confident in their truth. This support is how we can subvert the dominant narrative that has prevented innumerable people from living in their power and finding their tribe.

My challenge to you as you read through the rest of this chapter is to open yourself to the idea that all forms of familial connection are valid and that validity itself, whether reasonable or not, is not a concept to be subjectively undermined.

In late July 2010, I was freshly twenty years of age and at the height of my alt-Barbie princess heyday. I remember sweating profusely in the passenger seat of Angi's red Dodge Dakota, hurtling down Interstate 5, trying to keep a consistent signal while on a phone interview with Dan Savage.

Angi, Reed and I were headed to Eugene, Oregon, to attend Faerieworlds, a world music festival with a fairie theme. Summer was always a heavy festival season for my family; festivals were how my parents initially formed their bonds to one another. The tradition of packing up our costumes and camp gear and hitting the road to party our hearts out for the weekend was well established by the time I came around. The family worked hard to find time amid everyone's busy schedules and home-schooling Royce, Reed and me, once I dropped out of public school, to gather and celebrate the thing that had brought us all together. The theme of the festivals changed throughout the years, from medieval reenactment and Pagan retreat weekends to music festivals and sci-fi/fantasy conventions; as my parents grew older, they made sure to never lose their sense of adventure, instead deciding to invite my siblings and me into said adventure with them. We all happened to be giant nerds, so our adventures looked like us driving up and down the West Coast to festivals where we could connect with other counterculture families and celebrate being the wonderful weirdos that we are!

In addition to attending festivals, my tribe has also had a common thread of creating space for community to gather.

Later in the summer we would be attending the seventh year of
Polycamp Northwest, a camping weekend dedicated to polyamorous people, moresomes and families. Louise, one of my aunties in the tribe, had decided she wanted a camping event where
people could explore their polyamorous identity without any
other kind of theme overshadowing it. Polycamp was gaining
popularity in the Northwest, and Seattle's alternative newspa-
per *The Stranger* had agreed to do an article on the event. Dan
Savage had agreed to write the article, and they were looking for
interesting angles on the story. As the resident ham and lover of
attention in our family, I had offered my perspective as both a
second-generation polyamorous person and a polykid, and Mr.
Savage had taken the bait.

In my eccentric logistical fervor, I had booked the interview for the day that we were driving to Faerieworlds. Thus I
was shouting over the chorus of air conditioning and highway
rumble while my very patient mother and sibling sat quietly by,
shaking their heads and snickering at me. The interview had
been full of my fairly regular sound bites: "Mom taught me at a
young age we had to have a public face out in the world because
people wouldn't understand our family." And I shared how I had
to be careful which friends I brought to my house because of
how a friend's parents might react if they found out my parents
were sex-positive, polyamorous hippies.

Dan was trying to get a better sense of my family's structure and I, once again, began trying to explain the diagram of
my family without visual aid. I started with, "Well, my family's
polycule has changed several times throughout my life; right
now my bio-mom is living in a cross-quad and I live with
them—"

"Wait, did you just say polycule? What is that?"
Dan interjected.

It's a concept I had been prolifically talking about on LiveJournal, and I had gained a small amount of recognition for coining the term, with a variety of responses. Some people thought it was stupid and their way of explaining relationships was much more valid; others thought it was a brilliant way to describe things. Polyamorous people seem to love a good metaphor-based pun, and "polycule" hit the mark for them. I discerned from Dan's response that if I explained it well, I was fairly certain the concept would end up in the article and basically solidify me as the recognized creator of the term. That's what happens when you quote something catchy to a famous columnist, right?

I said, "When I was in high school, I was doing chemistry homework, totally frustrated because it didn't make any sense to me, and suddenly I had a shift. I thought about the molecules like they were people in a nonmonogamous relationship! The oxygen atom has a large desire for a partner and finds stability having four other atoms in its life and craves stability and being the focus of its partners. This works great for hydrogen, who needs a strong connection in its life to keep it grounded; elsewise it can be incredibly flighty. Hydrogen generally has a connection to another hydrogen that predates them getting together with oxygen. These two hydrogens understand each other and support their efforts in finding a grounding force who will help give them purpose. The charge the hydrogens feel when they find their oxygen is intense, and they bond instantly! Balancing the polar needs of the hydrogen takes up most of oxygen's focus, and all three find stability in their dynamic!"

"Uh-huh?" Dan agreed sarcastically. "So you're saying you once anthropomorphized your science homework and now that's what you use to describe your family's structure?"

I felt like I was losing him, so I quickly reframed my explanation. "Think about a molecule and the way it's structured. You have atoms, those are people, they have a charged attraction to other atoms, form bonds of different types, and the structures adjust based on those bonds. The bonds sometimes break, and the structure is adjusted," I stated confidently.

Dan said, "Oh, that's good. I like that." I smiled to myself. It was validating to be able to explain these complex concepts in a succinct way, considering half of the time I was basically flying off at the mouth. My theater background and experience with the media was paying off!

The interview went out within the week, and I began to receive a flurry of attention on the internet specifically regarding the term. Of all the things I was quoted saying about my childhood and experiences at Polycamp Northwest, the thing folks seemed to latch on to was the fact that I had either the wisdom or the audacity, depending on who was commenting, to label myself as the inventor of the term "polycule." People twice my age who felt entitled to sole credit for the term were raining their possessive opinions down on me, and I had no idea how to react. I was simply a teenager practicing molecular biology homework with my mom and sibling, and we found a solid metaphor to work with; why were folks getting so bent out of shape? I chose not to engage in the unnecessary power struggles with fellow nerds on LiveJournal; I knew better. My creation of the term "polycule" was as valid to me as the structure of my family; it's my internal truth, and in this case I wasn't actively looking for external validation to solidify that for me. I honestly hadn't heard anyone talk about the concept before I did and felt validated simply by using the term in my everyday life, which included doing so in the media. Little did I know then how bold of a choice that would turn out to be. The external response to my "invention" of the word has been varied, but does that make it invalid? I understand that in a globalized world with diversified platforms on which one can get their message out, people can simultaneously create identical concepts they successfully use in their microcosm. I always keep this in mind, and when I end up running into others who use an identical concept to one I hold dear in my life, I celebrate it and look at the experience as a way I can further connect with someone, engaging in co-creation (pun intended) instead of competition. Inevitably, we are all just trying to figure out ways to explain ourselves and receive external validation for such.

Adulting, Part Two: The Mouthpiece

I was a bundle of nerves, sitting there on the edge of the stage, staring out at the five-hundred-seat auditorium at the University of Washington's School of Medicine. The hall was full to the rafters with the chatter of students. The moderator was working with the sound person to set up the microphone, and Allena was furiously texting the other two panelists for our polyamory discussion. She always got more strict about us being on time and presentable when we spoke at the university.

Allena Gabosch was the executive director of the Center and Foundation for Sex Positive Culture. Most of the community called her "Mom." She was a powerhouse of a woman, fiercely femme, covered in tattoos and as jovial as she was fair. When I was seventeen, I had specifically asked her out for coffee to ask her advice about how to enter the same kink community that my parents were a part of. We took to each other's large personalities right away, and she'd been so honored I asked for her advice that we basically established a mentor/mentee relationship from the get-go. I worked as her executive assistant at the Center for several years and frequently spoke with her at local colleges on both polyamory and BDSM.

The panel started with us each introducing ourselves and a bit of our backstory, then opening the floor for questions. Inevitably, within the first two to three questions I would be asked about my experience growing up polyamorous. I felt it coming when the thirty-something male-presenting student took the mic, looked around somewhat hesitantly and then directly at me, stating, "This question is directed specifically at Koe. With your parents having so many relationships and people around all the time, were you exposed to sex at a young age?" I smiled; he was so earnest and eloquent, trying to be politically correct in front of all of these other people.

This student's question was essentially asking about how my own sexuality developed in a polyamorous household, but he was doing so in a way that wasn't totally drenched in sex negativity. It was a nice change, actually, since most people went straight for the phrasing "Did your parents ever do stuff, like, in front of you?" Which, beyond being a vaguely crude way of asking about sexuality in front of children, is an inquiry that obviously showcases a person's preconception that polyamory as a whole is inherently sexually boundaryless. Preconceptions like this conflate the idea of promiscuity with being sex positive.

Sex positivity is the viewpoint that sex and sexuality is a natural, regular part of one's life; it is not shameful or wrong and is able to be both celebrated and normalized. The value of providing a child with this access to experience their own sexuality, without shame, fundamentally gives them advantages in navigating numerous aspects of their adult life, including the ability to negotiate, their self-confidence and their comfort with engaging in their sexuality. These advantages combined with my personal love of the spotlight are precisely the reason that I was called on to do speaking gigs like these, and I was great at discerning what someone actually wanted to know and answering with a positive anecdote that made people laugh; which is exactly what I was about to do.

I felt Allena tense next to me. She had been speaking at colleges for sixteen years, and she was protective of who she invited to speak with her. She still remembered the very first time I joined her, five years ago, and how I brought up my sexual abuse as a child and derailed the whole class. Nowadays I knew better. I had perfected my soundbites through interacting with the drama-hungry media and knew which details were appropriate for public consumption and which were safer to keep to myself. I chuckled lightly to reassure Allena; I was going to make this a lighthearted answer, not to worry.

"Not all polyamorous parents or families choose to be out to their children about their love lives or are sex positive in the same way mine was, but I believe the concept of giving children age-appropriate information (discussed in more detail in Chapter Four) is a fairly ubiquitous concept in parenting. My parents were conscious of what they exposed me and my siblings to based on where we were at developmentally and what boundaries (also discussed in Chapter Four) we kids had. The level of public displays of affection they'd express in front of me and what kind of content I had access to was intentional. The difference is that sex as a concept wasn't hidden from me; it wasn't treated as wrong or shameful, it was an aspect of our lives that was normalized. The key was to introduce sexuality to us kids at age-appropriate levels, which we directed. Our parents set up a dynamic where we were able come to them with our questions about anything, including sex, and they would be answered honestly, to an age-appropriate degree. This way our parents would know what we were interested in and where we were at in our growth process. They would not share information that we didn't ask about unless there was a direct need for the information.

"For instance, when my wrestling with my brother got to be intense enough, our parents instilled boundaries that made sense and were appropriate to our behavior. Number one was no permanent damage. When I was continually whacking my brother in the balls, because it was hilarious to watch him fall over in pain, my parents stopped us and explained that my behavior could seriously injure my brother and his capacity to have children if he wanted to do so in the future and thus I needed to stop. They gave me the appropriate information for the moment; we did not stop to have a full conversation about testes' role in reproduction, I just knew that I needed to not injure my brother. Our parents also chose this circumstance to introduce the idea of safewords to us when we weren't listening to each other's sentiments of 'no' and 'stop' during our wrestling matches and tickling marathons. The parameters for a suitable safeword were that it was one syllable, easily said when you were gasping for breath, and it needed to be something that wasn't commonly said so it would be noticeable." I smiled again, letting the students know it was okay to laugh at the story.

The student followed up with, "But, did that really work?"

I couldn't tell if he meant the safewords or the dynamic as a whole. I chose to answer the former. "The safewords worked great and gave a tool for us kids to create our own boundaries with each other as we grew up versus going to our parents over every little dispute. Around the time my breasts were growing, my brother would give me purple nurples, which *hurt*!" A few snickers rippled throughout the crowd. I continued, "My brother said this was recompense for my whacking him in the balls so often. 'Turnabout is fair play!' he would say. When I went to my parents, I was reminded that I could use my safeword if I needed to, that's what it was there for. This was not the answer I wanted to hear, and my smug-faced brother was no help. He knew he'd been playing by the rules: I consented to engage in roughhousing, and if I wanted something different, I needed to negotiate. I swear, there is nothing worse than a gloating older brother, am I right?" Finally, a wave of laughter ran through the hall, and I felt Allena's strong clap on my upper arm as she chuckled heartily.

"Good job," she whispered to me.

3

"How Did You Make It All Work?"

"By sharing the responsibility amongst all the adults, both with the children as well as each other. It was just as important to have a good co-parenting dynamic as a mutual sounding board, venting partner and mediator, as it was to have a lover." –Angi

Adult on Deck

The term "Adult on Deck" comes from the nautical definition of the person who was on a shift working the deck of the ship. This dynamic allowed our parents to share responsibility equally and gave them space to be "off" for a while. The ability to clear their heads and be adults allowed them to come back to their children excited and refreshed! Having an Adult on Deck also allowed the parents to direct information through one source point and prevented the children from pitting the parents against each other as much. It didn't eliminate miscommunication, but it did facilitate us kids getting away with slightly less shit starting.

Functionally, the role of Adult on Deck was planned by the parents, who would negotiate a schedule as a part of our regular scheduling as well as prior to events; each parent would have an understanding of the general time frame that they were expected to be "on" and which kids they were overseeing. In the days before the life-saving technology of digital calendar sharing, if the adult needed to hand over the role to another parent for some reason, they would communicate either in person or via phone, and the polycule would support them in rearranging parental roles. If the change was made in advance, the children would be informed within twenty-four hours of the change in the schedule with statements like "Phoebe will be picking you up from school tomorrow and will be your Adult on Deck until Angi gets home." If the change needed to happen in the moment, then the person stepping into the Adult on Deck role would round up the children, generally with a loud shout of "Children, front and center!" with that parental tone indicating you did not have a choice but to be front and center, as soon as possible. You would hear the new plan, mirror it back, showing the adult that you understood, then went back to the game you had been so rudely taken away from.

Having an Adult on Deck was not only a tool to create clarity between the children and parents, but it also served a function in the greater community we were a part of. This was especially important at social events such as polyamorous potlucks, indie concerts fronted by bands composed of our community members or functions at our local Pagan church. There were commonly multiple families at these events with a high amount of crossover in polyamorous families present, so it became important for our community to have an efficient way for everyone to look out for everyone else. The kids were generally all running together as a pack, so we were given someone to check in with.

The dynamic worked for the most part, though there were a few circumstances in which the Adult on Deck model didn't work and needed to be re-evaluated in the moment. For instance, watching out for one another is a fine concept until you run into an adult assuming they have sovereignty over a child whom they have no connection with. One of my most deeply rooted pet peeves is an adult assuming familiarity with me. My siblings and I knew very distinctly who our parents, aunties/uncles and elders were, and if you were not a part of one of those categories, you were a community member.

Community members were to be treated with common courtesy and a generally jovial nature, but you did not have any obligation to take a directive from a community member unless it was associated with imminent danger. The community was built to look out for one another, and if you someone told you "Don't climb on that, it's not stable," common courtesy was to believe them. However, if you knew for a fact that what you were doing was allowed by your Adult on Deck and the individual trying to tell you differently was not a parent of yours, you had every right to go on as you were. Adults who tried to push the issue and be overbearing would get a talking-to by the parents—they're called boundaries for a reason!

The exceptions to this dynamic were as follows.

Running with the Pack: When you were a herd of kiddos running together, either there would be an Adult on Deck designated to look over the kiddos, or a group norm would be created for the pack that all of the kiddos adhered to. This norm might be different than the default set of rules in your family but was instituted to take everyone's levels of capacity and accessibility into account. If big kids wanted to go climb thirty-foot evergreens and smalls didn't know how to do that safely, you had to compromise on how to play all together.

Minion Duty: To be in the role of Minion was to be in helpful service to the community. This was a role that could be called on by a parent at any time for help with a particular task. Minion Duty could also be pre-assigned, and there would be chunks of time set aside for you to "Be a Minion," aka a helping hand.

Though generally mandatory, this kind of service was valuable to our parents and treated with respect. They explained to us that everyone in the tribe participated fully, at their own capacity, and to be a Minion meant you were participating in making life functional for all of us. You were never given a task that was outside of your capacity, and if you needed help, you were encouraged to ask for such. Minioning also had a rewards system built in, so you could barter Minion time for things such as shinies (luxury items) and often were rewarded with special experiences such as clothing sprees, movies or trips to the local water park.

When you were in a Minion role, you had a designated person or people you were taking direction from. These people may not have been your parents or aunties/uncles, but for the negotiated Minion duty, they were essentially your Adult on Deck. As a Minion, you still did not need to take directives from other adults who were not involved in the project you were helping with at the time. This was only overridden when the family's needs trumped the action at hand. For example, if I was Minioning for someone at a social event and my family was getting ready to leave, then I would be released from Minion Duty. (This concept may seem familiar to kinksters as "being in service," which is an aspect of dominance and submission. News flash: parent-child relationships are nonsexual Dominant/submissive relationships. I recommend treating them with as much intentionality and care as your other relationships.)

Sleepovers: When you were staying over at someone else's house, you had to follow the house's rules. The parent, adult or babysitter for the sleepover was the Adult on Deck, and you took directive from them while at their house. Parents would negotiate what a kiddo's access needs were before the sleepover so the child wouldn't be asked to do something that they were incapable of doing.

The dynamic worked within our community because there was mutual buy-in from both the parents and the children. If a child wasn't in a space where they could engage with an Adult on Deck, due to tiredness, anxiety or recalcitrance, the child would be directed back to their primary parent for care. Sometimes what you really need is to just deal with your own parent, and no one else will substitute.

It's also a dynamic that is easily understood by children. We kids knew exactly what it meant when our parents would tell us "Jim is your Adult on Deck until dinner," and we enjoyed the dynamic for the most part. We saw it as a bit of a game, trying to figure out what we could get away with based on which parent was the Adult on Deck. I remember multiple occurrences of me standing in the middle of the library at church shouting, "Who's the Adult on Deck for me right now?" at a decibel considered more appropriate for a rock concert, just to make sure my Adult on Deck was paying attention. I've always joked that I have a particular knack for putting the "b" in "subtlety."

As the Adult on Deck concept was something my parents were creating mostly out of thin air, it wasn't perfect, and it was constantly being reevaluated, particularly when we kids would poke holes in it. As a kid, when the most important information the Adult on Deck had was different from what your parents had told you—current groundings or restrictions, for example—emotional devastation would often rain down upon the

Adult on Deck. In these instances, the primary parent would be contacted to correct the misinformation. However, sometimes the primary parent could not be reached, so the Adult on Deck had to make the final decision; if the child could be calmed and reasoned with during this time, then you would discuss the differences in information and come to a compromise until the primary parent could be reached. If the child was spun up and could not be reasoned with, then the Adult on Deck would put their foot down, and their information would take precedence until the primary parent could be reached. At other times the issue would be the child trying to get what they wanted by manipulating the Adult on Deck and playing he said/she said/they said with the parents, which we called "splitting." When splitting was afoot, the dynamic of Running It Up the Flagpole came into play.

Running It Up the Flagpole

"Go Run It Up the Flagpole" is inarguably one of the top three most common phrases I heard growing up. It was introduced in my early childhood and was always available to us kids as a permissions tool. As we got older it became ingrained in us, and we generally didn't need the verbal reminder to initiate it. Running It Up the Flagpole meant that a kid needed to get different perspectives to see if their information or idea was sound; when you have more than two parents to bounce information between, it becomes important for the parents to have a system for keeping a united front when the kiddos came calling. As a counterbalance to all of the information coming through the Adult on Deck, Running It Up the Flagpole was a way for all of the parents to maintain a united front while still having their own perspectives and opinions. The parents would negotiate and agree on the boundaries laid out for the kids, and the Adult on Deck would lay out the ground rules for the children. Then we, as kids, had the option to run an idea past the parents if it came up, aka Run It Up the Flagpole, whenever we wanted to do something that wasn't directly outlined in the boundaries discussion given by the parents or the Adult on Deck.

My family used this strategy not only as a way for the parents to back one another up but also to help the children develop logical reasoning skills. Say you had a tremendous idea about wanting to have a water balloon fight two hours before you had to head out to a family function! After presenting the idea first to your primary parent or the acting Adult on Deck, you would then need to run the idea by at least one of the other assembled adults and get their perspective. Each adult would ask you a few questions about your logic and what the other adults had said. If you could present a solid enough argument for your idea and laid out how you were going to make it work, you would go back to the original parent asked or the acting Adult on Deck, present your final proposal, and then go forth and do it. About half of the time my water-balloon-filled dreams came true and the other half I wound up feeling very grumpy about "stupid adult logic," which is honestly a better ratio than I end up with nowadays as an actual adult.

The times this led to miscommunication were when the adults were out of alignment about the rules, special arrangements or restrictions the child was under at the time. There's also the inevitable game of telephone that happens when you're translating multiple pieces of information through a child. To help mitigate this, after the child had asked all of the parents and come back with the various answers they had received, if there wasn't consensus among the adults, they would deliberate and discuss their answers. A good example is a child asking for a spontaneous sleepover. If a parent was a No because they had plans early in the morning and weren't able to host or participate, the parents who were a Yes would be able to support the No parent by changing their answer to no. Conversely, if a parent who was a Yes had no conflicts or issues hosting, they could take on the responsibility, allowing the No parent to change their answer to yes, and they would move on to getting the logistics worked out.

When all of these tools failed and miscommunications arose, the original adult the child asked, whether it be the primary parent or Adult on Deck, would make the final decision, so there was an opportunity for said adult to go check in with the other adults and see where the breakdown in communication was.

My family knew we were creating new dynamics and didn't expect them to be perfect. We were continuously engaged with them, however, and didn't let our miscommunications get out of control, especially when the children were the focus of the communication. Sometimes the ambiguous information even worked in favor of us kids and we got away with things we probably shouldn't have, an occurrence my family commonly referred to as "yet another fucking learning experience."

Due to this potential for splitting, the children would receive accurate, transparent information with a focus on both negotiation and compromise. If a child could give a compelling and well-thought-out counterproposal to an adult's suggestion, it would be considered with the same weight the parent would give any tribe member and would be discussed with the other parents. This allowed the children to have a voice in the conversation while understanding the logic in what the parents were asking for. If the counterproposal was either totally illogical, according to stupid adult logic, or was not feasible for the current situation, instead of telling the child a flat-out no, the adult would compromise with the child, coming as close to a place of mutual satisfaction as they could. After all, it is vastly easier to deal with a child who receives some portion of what they want than one who is having feelings about being denied something, especially when they have made a perfectly reasonable request.

A common example of this was whenever our tribe had a social gathering, inevitably one and sometimes all of the kids would want to stay the night at the host child's house without having planned it in advance. We children who wanted to stay over would plot to each go to our primary parent, hands in a prayer position, bat our eyelashes and pout. The parent would smile and inquire, "Have you asked their parents?" We would shake our heads. The parent would say, "It's fine by me, but you need to go Run It Up the Flagpole." We would then spend the next half-hour tracking down all of our parents present at the party and get their okay. Each of the parents would be sure to use the same formula with the child, stating, "Have you asked your other parents? It's fine by me, go Run It Up the Flagpole." Eventually, the children would huddle up and report back about who could stay and who couldn't.

Simultaneously, the adults would have been checking in with one another to see if they were each receiving the same information from the children and if each parent had been using the flagpole formula. The flagpole formula is effective because it avoids splitting between parents and puts the impetus on the children to gather information about their request. When the child's question was unrealistic, the parent would start a line of reasoning with the child about why their request wouldn't work. Again using the example about spontaneous sleepovers: our tribe didn't all live in the same place, and some members lived upwards of an hour away in the suburbs of Seattle; they also happened to have the swankiest house, which we kids would naturally want to have sleepovers at. The following conversation happened between Angi and me more times than I can count before puberty:

Angi would listen intently and respond, "You're saying you'd like to stay over at Leigh's house tonight? Okay, what are you doing tomorrow?"

I'd think about it and say, "I have play rehearsal."

Angi would counter, "Right. So, how do you plan on getting home from Leigh's house in time to get ready for your rehearsal?"

I would offer brightly, "You could come pick me up!"

At this point, Angi would attempt not to raise her eyebrows too obviously and say, "That's an extra two trips for me to do early in the morning that I hadn't planned on, and I have David staying over tonight."

I distinctly remember that as soon I felt this conversation not going in the direction I desired, I would begin pouting with my arms crossed. "But everyone is going to cuddle and play video games, *and* there's gonna be pancakes for breakfast! Why do you get to have a sleepover and I don't?"

I've asked Angi how she would maintain patience at this point, and she said she would take a calming breath, remember she loved me and explain, "Because David and I have had our sleepover planned for a week. If you and Leigh would like to plan a sleepover for another night, we can certainly talk to Leigh's parents about that."

Knowing me, my pout would intensify by several notches and Angi would recognize I was heading towards tantrum territory and wasn't going to be able to hear adult logic right now, so she would instead offer a compromise. "How about this: in the morning, you, David and I can cuddle and then make pancakes for breakfast before rehearsal?"

My love of pancakes was deep and pure as a child, and thus my eyebrows would begin to unknit themselves, my fists would soften their death grip and the pout would drop. "Okay, I guess..."

Angi learned early on not to take my shit and would call out my bluff. "We don't have to have pancakes if you don't want—"

"No! I want pancakes!" I would exclaim, reaching desperately towards Angi.

She would then smile and say, "Great! Do you want to go talk to Leigh's parents about setting up a sleepover soon?"

To which I would nod and say, "Yes, please."

This way, everyone got what they wanted, just maybe not in the way they were expecting at the time.

Trans-parent-cy

The impetus for this book came from a desire to answer the numerous questions I receive about the building blocks that made my family's polyamorous dynamic work. Thus far, I have covered tools we used to make things run more smoothly. What I would like to do now is take a look at the value of parental transparency, a dynamic so fundamental in its influence that I didn't fully realize how much it affected my parental relationships until I sat down to write this book.

The philosophy is simple: be transparent with children so they will see you as a full-fledged human who they will want to be transparent with in return. As part of maintaining an environment where I was safe enough to come to my parents with any and all of my questions, they worked diligently on being open and honest with me about both their parental logic and their feelings.

This is not to say they shared with me to the point of irresponsibility; they continued to frame their transparency through age appropriateness, making sure they weren't imposing a level of emotional labor on me that I wasn't ready for. They were also in the process of dismantling their programming about transparency in parenting, taking the pieces that worked for them and finding balance between the parental archetype as the stable authority figures they had grown up with and their mutual desire to be in vulnerable partnership with me.

When I asked Angi about her experience with this, she responded, "As a child, I saw a difference in how I interacted with my mother and with my peers. I have always considered my mother to be one of my best friends. I have been able to maintain a level of emotional connection with her throughout all of these years based on mutual vulnerability, and I wanted to have that with my child." Angi came from a more traditional upbringing and was always thinking about which aspects of her upbringing she wanted to impart to me. She initially wanted to disregard all authoritative dynamics she experienced in her own upbringing, but as she grew in her parenting, having to deal with a smart, willful child, she began to find value in some of the traditional dynamics her parents had imparted to her. She was also not raising me in a vacuum, and her idea about what good parenting dynamics looked like needed to be congruent with what the parents, as a whole, had agreed was the best way to raise the children. She had to make some compromises about what to engage with from her past and the future she was building with her children and co-parents.

At its core, the idea of transparency is to be free of pretense or deceit and instead be readily understood. This concept is considered a cornerstone of ethical nonmonogamy but is not always so readily associated with traditional parenting models in modern Western culture. Let's look at the phrase "because I said so," a sentiment I find to be a lazy, common catch-all response for questions about answers that parents don't want to be questioned on. The phrase itself is inexplicit and more a demonstration of power over a child than a thoughtful consideration of their inquiry. Even when the child is asking a question that the parent is unwilling to answer, there are ways in which a parent can be open about why their answer is not going to satiate the child's thirst for information. This is an act that in itself shows the child that the adult is still present with them, even if the child isn't getting exactly what they want. The obscurity of the statement "because I said so" creates a barrier directly between the parent and child, and with regular use it has the potential to breed resentment as the child grows.

Throughout my childhood, instead of "because I said so," I would receive age-appropriate answers to my questions that were rooted in truth but did not give away more details than I was able to grasp at the time. For example, I often had burning questions that Angi wasn't able to give the proper space and context to answer to my satisfaction, like "How is an XXX video different than a regular video?" She would say, "I can see this is important to you, and we don't have time to discuss it in detail right now. Can you please trust me and the information I'm giving you? I promise I will give you all of the details when I can." In these moments, Angi was sharing with me that she cared about my question and knew me well enough to know that I was not going to take well to receiving a subpar answer, so she was offering a compromise wherein I would be able to get what I needed, while being truthful about her capacity in the current circumstance.

Logistics are an excellent example of how transparency can be used as a tool for negotiating with children, but I find the most valuable part of transparency comes with the vulnerability that parents choose to share with their children. Simply put, vulnerability brings parents and children closer together. Choosing to show vulnerability to children, whether it be mental or emotional, means you are actively modeling to the children that they can be vulnerable with you in return.

This is not to say that you need to share every single detail of your inner monologue with a child. It is especially important to exercise your boundaries regarding what you are open to sharing with children, based on what you have mutually decided is appropriate. When my parents needed to talk about things they either felt was inappropriate for us kids or simply didn't want to have to explain in depth, particularly regarding their relationships, they would simply say, "This is adult conversation and doesn't concern you. Go ahead and have kidlet time while we have adult time." Even when this response felt exclusionary in some way, it was a known dynamic where kids got the privilege of being kids and the parents got the privilege of having adult time. The parents would also frequently remind us that their conversation was likely to bore us to tears and we would have much more fun going outside to play anyway.

Through this dynamic, each of our roles as parent or child were well defined, and thus we could each flesh out how we wanted to engage in said role. Each individual was able to build trust with the other members of our family in their own way, meaning that though no two parent-child relationships looked the same, we all were also able to actively engage in choosing what family meant for us. This is the same concept some non-monogamous folks use to build the relationship that works best for them, using the same building block idea we covered in

"Ergonomic Relationships" in Chapter Two. The difference here is that we are using it in the context of a polyamorous family versus an adult-adult relationship.

Transparency's direct value for children shows up not only when the child feels empowered by witnessing the thought processes of mom, dad, daddy and mum, but when the child begins engaging in transparent conversations with the parents in return. I've found this to become increasingly more important as the child grows into adolescence and engages in secrecy as a method of exercising control over their autonomy. By giving the child continued access to information they desire, they have less reason to create a narrative about your actions, your reasoning and judgment of your character based on the narrative they have created. Every lie I told my parents came from my desire to evade the fair consequences of my actions; I attempted to lie, but it wasn't truly necessary and often unsuccessful. I came to realize that I didn't need to lie to my parents about anything, because my parents didn't lie to me.

The act of lying was seen as an act of manipulation and was the most severely punished misbehavior in my family. Therefore, the act of lying satisfied the thrill I was looking for; I wanted to explore the act of deception more than I actually needed to keep details from any of my parents or siblings. In my exploration, other than discovering I was not very good at deception, I found that engaging in my communications with transparency allowed me to take responsibility for my actions, get less punished than I would have had I lied, and be able to make decisions about how I would like to engage with the consequences of my actions. I also found it straight-up stressful to keep up the lie with so many parents' skills of deduction to contend with—the boon of polyamorous parenting had struck again!

I understand that this concept may seem idealistic, and its success rate is inevitably not going to look exactly the same for each child you engage with. There is also the looming question "What happens when you end up sharing too much information with the child? Will it ruin them for life?" Short answer: Ruin? No. Change significantly? Maybe.

Remember that your influence in a child's life is powerful—use your powers for good!

Humans are resilient, even privileged ones, and children will continue to grow, change and evolve throughout their entire life. You may end up affecting the child's internal landscape if you are around during a fundamental time, but that's also the natural consequence of being a part of a child's life.

Angi often wonders if she gave too much information on her emotional state when I was a young child. To this, I respond that though there were moments of shock involved in seeing my parent grieve a partner or make difficult financial decisions, I was grateful that she was sharing these moments with me so that I was able to help take care of both myself and her, in the ways that I could, throughout the course of my life. I encourage you to never underestimate the power of a solid cuddle session from a determined snuggle monster in your time of strife. Letting the children in your life use their wisdom to comfort you is a sign that you trust them and their ability to help. As with all of the offerings I share throughout this book, they are meant to be taken with consent and moderation in mind. There is always going to be a line where the information you share may be too much for the child to handle; it's important to always consider age appropriateness when choosing when and how you share yourself with the children in your life. Ease children into situations, and turn the dial up on sensitive content slowly and steadily; make sure to balance your approach, as children are sponges and will imprint what you are demonstrating to them faster and more deeply than you will anticipate.

In my years of publicly presenting, I have been accused many times of sugarcoating my experiences as a second-generation sex-positive polykid. To this, I honestly admit I highlight the more positive aspects of my childhood because of the value those experiences have brought me as an adult. My choosing to focus on positivity does not mean I didn't have struggles in my upbringing around how my family chose to engage in everyday sex-positive polyamory with us kids around.

———

Before puberty, I was generally fairly ambivalent about sex noises because my parents had been incredibly good about practicing their intimacy in a way that didn't affect me negatively. However, by the time I hit fourteen, I was already a raging sex geek with no sexual partners who was just coming off of a personal modesty phase. Gary and his fiancée were deep in NRE (new relationship energy) and exploring BDSM, and Angi was having a resurgence of her sex drive. I feel it important to mention that the walls of our house were quite thin, and for some inexplicable reason the heating ducts went directly from my father's room to mine. We were the perfect storm of misaligned needs; I needed them to be understanding about teenage hormonal onslaught and they needed me to be understanding about them getting their freak on.

Essentially, I became a raging ball of judgment. I spewed sex negativity towards both Angi and Gary for the fact that they were putting their sexual desires ahead of my basic well-being. Even after we had all talked and set up boundaries about when and how my parents would behave, the sound of their sexuality had become a trigger for me, and any time I began to hear it, even within our boundaries, I would become irate and generally hate the world for being able to have sex when I felt I couldn't. I struggled with this feeling throughout my teens, and when I began to explore with my partners, I would force myself to be quiet as a kind of personal protest against the onslaught I felt my parents were putting me through. I knew there was nothing inherently wrong with the sex they were having, but I felt like they were throwing it in my face, their lack of discretion showing enough of a lapse in respect that it was hard to show them any respect in return. This conflict came to a head during an event my family has come to call XXXMas 2009.

It was December 25th, 2009. Our holiday festivities had wound down, and by 9 p.m. the family would have normally been cuddled together, watching a movie. Instead, my sibling Reed and I had sequestered ourselves in my bedroom at the top of the large polyamorous house I was living in, in an attempt to get as far away from the chorus of eroticism as we could get without leaving the property. As any reasonable teenagers would do (I was nineteen, Reed was fourteen), we had taken the last of the yuletide desserts with us, an act of rebellion against those who were deciding that getting some was the best way to wind down our holiday celebration instead of being present with us, the youngest members of the tribe.

Each house member had a partner sleeping over: my brother Royce and his girlfriend were necking in the hot tub, Reed's parents were having a threesome in the den, and Auntie Louise was topping a BDSM scene in the living room to get her partner into a submissive headspace so Angi could pierce their nipples in the kitchen. Reed and I sat morosely in my room, eating homemade chocolate truffles, drinking Martinelli's apple cider and watching old sci-fi movies at an unreasonable decibel to try to drown out the noise.

The movies weren't doing the trick, and my sugar high was compounding my sexual frustration to the point that I just... kind of lost it. I looked at Reed and said, "Want to go throw snowballs at Royce and his girlfriend from the upper deck?" Reed's face lit up like, well, a kid on Christmas Day, and we dashed to my bedroom door. We snuck along the deck, which had a perfect view of the hot tub below, and scooped huge handfuls of snow off of the railing. We packed the ice loosely to make sure it would splatter all over the two of them, and on a silent count of three, let our frozen presence be known. As soon as we heard the girlfriend shrieking, we dashed back to my room, closed the door and collapsed laughing.

Within moments, I was leaning my full weight against my bedroom door as Royce was trying to force his way into my room, yelling obscenities at the both of us. He eventually overpowered me and made his way into the room, where I laughingly tried to brush off what Reed and I had done. "Hey, you know that sex isn't allowed in the hot tub," I said.

Royce wasn't in the frame of mind to hear my reasoning and responded by grabbing my hair and dragging me to the ground, saying, "That's not what we were doing, and you know it."

I attempted an elbow to the groin, saying, "That's not what I saw!" He blocked the groin, but I was able to cut him off at the knees, and we began brawling. Reed was on the bed, telling us to knock it off and that we were both being stupid.

My actions got all three of us in trouble. Royce and me for fighting, and Reed for throwing the snowball. The parents hadn't cared a lick about Royce and his girl snogging in the hot tub, which I was furious about. My parents cared far more that I had chosen sex negativity and violence to express my feelings and dealt with those issues directly in punishment.

The reason I share this particular story is not to condemn any one person; we all had our moments of choice that led us to action and subsequent consequence. My parents, making sure the overt sexual acts were taking place out of sight of the children, chose to lean into the sensual energy wafting through the house. Royce and his girlfriend were choosing to engage with each other in a way that felt safe for them, away from anything our parents were doing.

I was jealous and frustrated and acted out of anger that I had been fueling for eight years; I chose to take my feelings out not on my parents but on my brother, who was finally getting to enjoy being a part of the sex-positive culture our family had built in a way that felt safe for him. In retrospect, he had every right to be angry with me and ask for an apology. I also understand how his being that revved up would easily transmute into fury towards the sister who had been cockblocking him since he was a preteen.

It was a moment, however, where I questioned my parents' judgment about how much sexuality they were exposing us kids to, all at once. Even if we weren't in the room with anyone, we couldn't escape the experience. We were inundated with the sounds coming from every direction and became understandably overwhelmed. Though our family had been building dynamics for safe sex-positive expression for decades, we were still susceptible to mistakes like XXXmas.

As you develop the dynamics that work best for your family, however it's shaped, it is my hope that you will consider how much you want to show up, particularly as a parent, including the style of age-appropriate transparency you might want to take with the children in your life.

Adulthood, Part Three: Now, the Ugly

By the time my twenty-first birthday rolled around, it was clear to my mother's polycule that I was not making very much progress towards my life goals of becoming a full-time, financially stable sex educator. I was nowhere near to moving out of the house, and something needed to give. I had fallen from the alt-Barbie pedestal I had been residing upon and was suffocating in a pit of a depressive quagmire. I had developed a stress-based chronic illness that kept me from being able to keep up with my household obligations, and my marijuana use was affecting the entire household's mood. I had trapped myself in the nightmare of my internalized failure and was using marijuana as a catchall fix for my physical and emotional pain. I hadn't been able to hold a steady job in over a year, my homeschool studies had diminished to nothing and I was generally a passive-aggressive grump monster who ran off on adventures as often as I could.

In retrospect, I see how the rest of the household interpreted my actions as lazy and ungrateful. Storm's long-term partner Gina, my mother's metamour, was particularly unnerved by my actions. Gina had never appreciated the way I questioned the actions of the adults in the household, believing instead that, as Angi's child, I shouldn't have full say in household decisions. When Angi's disabilities affected her ability to work, my focus shifted to helping Angi instead of finishing my schooling or getting a full-time job, thus not contributing to the household financially. In Gina's mind, I was mooching off of the household, and she felt used. I felt as if I was watching someone else's life through a window in my mind. No matter how much I screamed at myself to make different choices, my general melancholia numbed me enough to the interactions I was having with the people I was living with that I couldn't muster the care or compassion to engage respectfully.

My conflict with Gina was an aggressive accelerant exacerbating the sudden tension of the household's polycule. The quad was destabilizing, and with some relationships having ended, the four adults were finding themselves divided into self-focused factions instead of leaning in to find solutions. The entire house generally felt like a minefield we were all tiptoeing through, and our bouts of drama were mounting, with frequent shouting matches adding fuel to the venomous rumors and doublespeak infiltrating our everyday communications. It seemed only a matter of time before someone stepped on the land mine that would dismantle everything we'd been working to build for six years. We had created a collective monster, and it was eating us alive; having forgotten our collective vision, each of us was reacting out of our own self interest, and no one was taking responsibility for their actions.

This was the most intense communication breakdown of a polycule I had ever witnessed firsthand, and I couldn't take it. In addition to being unable to successfully handle adulthood, I was finally old enough to feel like a full-fledged member of my tribe and was greeted to the experience by my elders blatantly showing me the darkest sides of their polyamory. My innocence about polyamory being consistently happy and successful was shattered, and I was heartbroken. I smoked to avoid the toxicity I was stewing in, and consequently the literal stench of my coping method was driving the household over the edge.

My mother's partner Storm ended up being the de facto patriarch of our household, no matter how much he desired extended network–style, egalitarian polyamory. He was the eldest, owned the house we lived in, had numerous lovers within our tribe and had a knack for creating community spaces.

During our house's descent into disharmony, he had been the one to maintain neutrality as best he could, choosing to hold on to hope that we would find resolution.

Neither Gina nor I were in the best of health, and once it became clear that we were making ourselves sick with the amount of stress our fighting was causing, everyone knew it was time for something to change. The decline in both my health and Gina's health was the breaking point for the house, and it was decided that one of us had to go. Gina had moved to Seattle with Storm ten years earlier, she had helped choose the beautiful house we all lived in, and though her health was steadily in decline, she was still managing to maintain a job and contribute to the household financially. In spite of Angi's persistent protest, I was the obvious choice to leave.

It fell upon Storm to have the conversation with me, as he was the most neutral party in the house. Storm and I sat across from each other in the household's overcrowded office, surrounded by stacks of file folders and the whir of aging computers. It was the one place in the house we could not maintain order and most always looked like the nest of several very nerdy albatrosses.

I knew it was a serious moment because Storm was having difficulty maintaining eye contact, a rare occurrence for him. I knew what was coming, but I continued to let him stumble through his recap of all the terrible bickering that had been happening around the house of late. This man had become as close to me as any of my blood family, and he had provided me wisdom and security for the past six years. We had shared laughter, adventure and clothing; I stole costumes out of his closet so often we had a running joke that it was because he had the body of an eighteen-year-old girl. He was my family. I loved him and didn't want him to suffer watching the loving family he had desired his entire life tear itself apart. So why wasn't I stopping him and telling him I would just pack up my stuff and go?

Because I was terrified and resentful; as far as I had seen, he hadn't done anything to quell the arguments between me and Gina. He had done nothing to support me through the emotional bullshit I was receiving from her, and now he was going to kick me out without a job or enough money to make it on my own? I had never lived on my own and felt so disconnected from my tribe at that time that I didn't know where I was going to go. I sat there, frozen in my fear and nodded along with him while looking resolutely at the dull blinking lights of the Wi-Fi router. My gaze jumped back to him when he said, "I know this mustn't be easy for you either. I want to let you know that I still think of you as a wonderful person. You are intelligent and creative, and it has been a blessing to be able to watch you grow up over these years. I have every faith that you will be able to find a way to succeed in building the life of your dreams."

His sapphire eyes were misty as he stared directly into my eyes, and I could not tell which I wanted to do more: slap him in the face or break down sobbing.

I fought back the tears welling up in my eyes, feeling the need to show him my strength and said, "Thank you for all that you have done for me; I didn't mean to be such a drain on you all. I'll need a week or two to figure out where to go and then will be out of your hair." He said there was no need to rush, to which I raised an eyebrow in response; we both knew that the sooner I was gone, taking myself out of direct contact with Gina, the sooner she would calm down. He offered a hug and I took it, using every ounce of willpower I possessed not to break down on his shoulder.

I drove to Gary's house right away and waited for him to get home from work. He arrived to find me huddled into a ball on the couch, weeping into the dusty caftan that lived on the back of the loveseat. He crossed the room with a bewildered "Oh, honey..." and scooped up in his arms. One of the things I have always appreciated about having a father over six feet tall is his capacity to make me feel small when I need it. We soon realized he was getting none of my story as I sobbed it into his chest, so we curled up on the couch and he asked me what was wrong.

I recounted how bad things had gotten at my house and how afraid I was about becoming homeless. He stopped me, saying, "Let's get one thing straight right now: as long as I have a roof over my head, I don't care if I have to convert the garage into a living space, you will have a place to call home. I currently have a newly empty room in the house, which you can move into right away, so you have nothing to worry about there. You will eventually find a job, and once you do, we can start talking about rent. It's okay, sweetie, this is what family is for, and I am happy that you came to me first. I love you." I remembered in that moment that my dad is, hands down, the best pep-talker on the planet, period. He had offered his space to me, without judgment, before I could even ask him. I was going to be okay. I had somewhere to go that was safe and some time to figure out what came next.

I was so vulnerable in that moment that I said, "Thank you, Daddy," as he kissed my forehead. I hadn't called him that since I was thirteen, when I was deep in the throes of puberty. It was around the time he was getting more active in the kink scene, and I was beginning to explore BDSM privately with my girlfriend. We both realized it felt weird for me to call him something that could be misconstrued by everyone around us as an erotic power dynamic, and I have intentionally called him either "Dad" or "Father" ever since. In this moment, though, there was no one else around, and what I really needed was him to be the person who had been cradling me, safe in his arms, since I was an infant. He held me with my back to his chest and gently rocked me, exactly the same way he had always done when soothing me from my nightmares about floating into outer space and never coming back. His deep, rumbly baritone hummed my childhood lullaby until my tears finally subsided and I fell asleep with my head in the crook of his neck.

4

"When Do the Kids Get to Just Be Kids?"

"We were constantly identifying and setting careful boundaries for the children: time boundaries, scheduling, space, exposure to metamours and choosing age-appropriate levels of information. This is how we kept you safe and let you be kids." –Gary

Tiny Humans

It's 1993. A father is meandering through the grocery store accompanied by a tottering, party-sized bag of tortilla chips with a pair of bright blue eyes peeking over the top, trying to see where she was going. Apparently, I had asked Gary if I could help carry some groceries, and when I refused all of the heavier items he tried to hand me, we compromised on a bag of chips as tall as I was. Though barely able to maneuver at more than a snail's space, I was determined to help out, and this bag of chips had become my sole responsibility. As we approached the deli counter, the deli clerk looked down and asked my father, "Well, isn't that adorable; did she ask to do that herself?"

Gary responded, "Yes!" and then looked down to me and said, "Honey, you are being very responsible about carrying groceries right now."

The clerk looked disbelievingly at my father and said, "Yeah, like she knows what that means." Gary raised an eyebrow and looked back to me, adjusting my grip on the poofy monstrosity I was carrying.

He asked me, "Honey, what does 'responsible' mean?"

I apparently thought about it for a moment and replied, "'Responsible' means being a good girl and helping your daddy when he asks for it."

Gary beamed as hard as a new father could and looked back to the deli clerk, whose mouth had fallen open in surprise. Looking back to my father, she asked, "How old is your daughter?"

Gary kept a straight face as he said, "Three, going on thirty-five." This anecdote was one of my father's favorite stories to recount to me growing up, highlighting the eloquence he focused on teaching me but also instilling the idea that our family was invested in teaching the children from a young age that we were strong and valuable members of the family.

People often commented on how the children were given responsibilities, which the commenter would question with either curiosity or judgment: "You let your kids walk to kindergarten by themselves? Isn't that dangerous? What if they get hurt?" My parents each had a different way of responding to this, fluctuating greatly in their level of graciousness, but all of them made sure to inform the commenter that our family ran under the apparently radical idea that children are "Tiny Humans" fully capable of expressing their limits, needs and capabilities and should be treated with respect based on our actions and requests. My mother Jean specifically avoided using baby talk with us as infants, especially as we were developing our speech patterns. It was important to her that we be able to communicate our needs accurately and effectively. This kind of logic continued throughout our upbringing, as our capabilities were judged based on our attitude and effort, not how long we had been breathing on the planet. From infancy through puberty we were regarded as Tiny Humans, affectionately nicknamed "Smalls" by Phoebe, Jean and Jim. The responsibilities we were entrusted with as Smalls focused primarily on being autonomous with our bodies: how to keep ourselves out of imminent danger and building routines such as hygiene and getting up for school.

Once we reached puberty, my siblings and I were referred to as "Adults in Training," and our developmental lessons started to focus on independence and external responsibility. Specifically, we were being taught how to take care of our environment, which manifested in such tasks as staying home alone, more complex household chores and eventually learning to drive. Becoming a fully active member of the tribe was another distinct hallmark of a child's growth into an Adult in Training; when you were able to handle complex negotiations and logistics, you would then be able to help with organizing tribal events. Having your perspective and voice given weighted consideration by your elders was a form of privilege the Adults in Training received, which was balanced by the responsibilities we were given as role models for the Tiny Humans of the tribe. We were not always stoked by all the various responsibilities of Adults in Training and, of course, would occasionally rebel against what our parents expected of us.

My siblings and I tended to be creative about our rebellion, and if we were being "smart little shits" as all of my mothers have recounted to me over the years, then we would be treated in such a fashion. How we were treated was a direct reflection of our behavior, because sometimes you are just not able to be a mature and functionally communicative human, particularly when you are flooded with sensory input and raging hormones. All of the responsibilities my parents bestowed were chosen based on our age-appropriate framework, and they did not expect us to take on tasks outside of our capability. My parents are tried and true nerds; they researched their faces off when it came to developmental stages, cognitive function and emotional intelligence. They kept in mind the external factors we were dealing with as kids and paid close attention to our attitude and the effort we put into different kinds of situations. If we were totally jazzed about doing something in particular, our parents would support our continued engagement with it. If we were struggling with something, our parents would confer about the best way to help us and develop a plan around which parent would take point on aiding the child and how the other parents would support. This was one of those times where it was extremely valuable to have numerous invested adults with a variety of skills available, both to share the load of supporting multiple children and to have diverse engagement styles that suited particular issues. Additionally, when one parent's engagement style or relationship with the particular child wasn't proving successful, another adult could step in.

Our fellow siblings were an additional resource we were used to drawing on when we needed help. There is a long-standing joke in my family that my brother Royce and I are the mathematical reciprocal for one another. We balance each other's challenge points with our strengths and have been able to fill in knowledge gaps for the other. He is a natural debater who is thirsty for information and has always joyously engaged in structured intellectual discourse with whomever is up to the challenge at the time. In contrast, I have developed a passion for emotional intelligence and exploring the esoterica of people's identities. It's not to say that we each don't possess the qualities the other excels at; we are still the tried and true nerds our parents raised us to be. Our divergent interests have led us to continue to be able to learn from one another, and a good chunk of our communication nowadays is about how to deal with interpersonal situations that require the other's strengths.

I need to make a clarification here about individualism. Though I've been explaining the dynamics my family raised us with as all-encompassing concepts, each of my siblings and I were seen as distinct individuals with different strengths and experiences that were shaping our prospective capabilities. The way our parents engaged in implementing age-appropriate responsibility and privilege was directly based on each child's interest, attitude and effort. By the time my brother Royce was seven years old, he was taking public transit by himself, primarily because he had been riding the bus with Jean since he was a Small. He was familiar with bus-riding etiquette, knew how to watch for signs of danger and proved he could be trusted to get off at the right destination. Angi and Gary primarily used cars to get around, so at that time I hadn't had the experiences that would have readied me to be a successful transit rider. Therefore, even though Royce and I are the same age, I wasn't given the same level of privilege and subsequent responsibility as him. This also comes down to a fundamental difference in parenting styles. Jean has always been a parent who assumes a child is fully capable, will make their own mistakes and will let you know when something is too difficult. Angi started as a parent who was constantly looking for ways to avoid hardship for her children; she didn't coddle us, we worked hard and learned tough lessons, but Angi also reacted from a place of new-parent paranoia, particularly when came to her only biological "gorgeous, blue-eyed, blonde-haired baby girl." I later found out that when I started middle school and began using transit to get across town, Angi had either herself or Jean follow the metro bus route all the way to my destination the first couple times I rode alone to make sure I was safe.

Throughout my childhood, Angi worked with this anxiety and released some of her fear, sometimes through being confronted head-on with her worst nightmare involving me and both of us turning out okay. When I called her from a small ravine off the freeway, after careening her beloved red pickup truck through the large sign reading "I-90 West to Seattle," I said, "I'm sorry Momma, this is the call I was never supposed to make to you. I crashed the car, I think it's totaled."

Her immediate response was "Are you okay?" I told her I thought so; I had been driven off the road by another car and was in shock, but the police were present and I had refused an ambulance. She responded with, "I can replace a car. I can't replace a child. Deep breaths baby, I'll be right there." The car was a goner, but I had come out with only a couple deep bruises, and she had faced one of her worst fears and now knew what was on the other side. I wasn't without consequence for crashing her truck, but I had been honest with her all the way through the experience and I was taking responsibility for my actions, which she held a lot of respect for.

Just like when you are creating a positive working polycule, the focus on maintaining open and honest communication between the parents and the children was one of the cornerstones of what made a great many of our family dynamics actually work. We were always a family that valued honesty more than we worried about mistakes, and my parents punished a lie two to three times more severely than whatever we were initially in trouble for. My siblings and I were taught that honesty is of the utmost importance. The act of being honest with our parents showed them that we were able to be people of integrity, to own our mistakes and be willing to take on the consequences of our actions. To directly quote Angi, "Most of the time when people lie it's because they don't want to pay the consequence." On an interpersonal level, lying was seen as a breach of that integrity and thus the ability to trust each other. On a logistical level, when we lied to our parents and elders, we were taking away their capacity to help us fix the problem or make things right. When lying came up as an Adult in Training, your importance as a role model was made particularly apparent.

One conversation with my mothers on the subject included the statement "As a role model for the youngers, your actions are seen and judged by others, not only by us parents, but other tribe mates as well as the larger community. These actions reflect not only on you but on the kids as a whole. The youngers will emulate your behavior, and think of how it would feel if they started lying to you?"

It was overwhelming, the thought that not only were my actions seen and judged by my immediate family, but that I was a representative of polyamory to the rest of our community and, to a certain extent, the world! It was a lot for a teenager to hold, and I didn't always succeed at being the best role model. The pressure to rebel was great. I would get tired of the responsibility and would lean into the age-old curse of youth: sweet, boundary-pushing hubris! I did lie, I snuck out, I actively showed Reed highly inappropriate hentai and generally tried to cover my tracks when I knew I was being a "bad kid." And you know what? Turns out I was pretty terrible at rebelling; I never tried for things that would permanently screw up my future, I was crap at lying to my parents and ended up telling them fairly soon afterward, and I never found I needed to reject those major identity labels that I happened to share with them (poly, kinky, sex-positive, etc.). The system of responsibility and privilege my parents had instilled was based on cause and effect, and despite my best teenage efforts, I was still generally being responsible and critical about my decisions. I was a successful Adult in Training after all, faults included.

As I have grown into the adult I am today, I have found a couple of ways these teachings have manifested. In general, my siblings and I were taught that we are not solitary organisms, but that we are part of an interconnected ecosystem where every organism has a function and the rest of the ecosystem is affected by the performance of the organisms within it. It's meta, I know, but this teaching generally did us a lot of good in regard to being conscious about our actions and engaging compassionately with others.

On the flip side, I've also found the continued focus on "the greater good" we received has instilled a deep and sometimes irrational sense of responsibility in me: the responsibility to be the most honest and noble polyamorous person I can possibly be, towards not only my partners and local sex-positive, poly-amorous community, but as a poster child for the polyamorous movement on the whole! This sense of spearheading accompanied by my love of the spotlight has led me to bill myself as a visible second-generation sex-positive and polyamorous icon. This sense of responsibility fueled the very drive that led me to write this book.

In my personal life, this has occasionally become a point of tension in moments where I make a significant mistake in my relationships. I begin to feel the weight of the multiplicitous parental teachings and disappointment I've fabricated for myself. I succumb to the feeling of failure as an ethical, polyamorous role model and allow myself to be swallowed by my self-imposed grief, not allowing my partner to express their reactions without compounding my emotional martyrdom. At these times I need to remind myself that I am more than the sum of my tribe's projected ideals and that everyone makes mistakes. It is not solely on my shoulders to make sure polyamory is seen as a perfect relationship structure with no flaws. I have been fortunate in my young adulthood to have had partners who have sat with me through this process. They have given me the harsh reality checks I've needed, by reminding me that the responsibility isn't all on my shoulders and that I don't have to always be what we have fondly dubbed the "The Atlas for Polyamory."

I know one thing I need to work on is the ability to take off my hat as a "fountain of knowledge" and be present in my own experience with my polyamorous identity. While I know I am polyamorous of my own volition, I also need to acknowledge that my conditioning as a polykid undeniably affects how my polyamorous identity was formulated. Though I do not consider this a negative, it is another piece of the puzzle within the greater picture of how my parents' eccentric influence impacted me and what I am doing about it now, as a full-fledged adult.

Age Appropriateness

One of the secrets to the success of my upbringing was something I find to be intrinsic in all child rearing: age appropriateness. As your child grows, they can handle increasingly complex information, but it's your job as an adult in their life to help them figure out what level of complexity is right for them, at the time. Due to the inherently complex nature of our family structure, my parents put a lot of focus on age appropriateness and commonly discussed it with us. This is also how they would frame conversations that the youth or even the parents were not ready to have. If there was a concept that they felt was too far out for where our development was, they gave us the age-appropriate version of the information as a way to give all of us some time before tackling the subject at its full complexity. Around four years old, I learned that babies come from a mother's tummy, when I was nine I learned the difference between the vagina and the urethra, and during puberty I learned about ovaries and fallopian tubes. Each time I came to my parents with more questions about the subject, I would get more details and be asked if they made sense. And when I got confused from asking too many questions, I would be told to go munch on what I had just learned and come back tomorrow if I wanted to know more.

This dynamic is one that sounds simple but takes discipline, like exercise! You, as the adult, continually encourage the children to come to you with any question or piece of information they would like to share. The trade-off is that the adult will always be open and nonjudgmental of the child when they are sharing. To achieve this, you must be able to free yourself from external judgment and control your knee-jerk reactions. Therefore, it is crucial that you acknowledge your triggers and learn to sit with discomfort, because if there is one thing children are good at, it's pushing your boundaries!

Like any form of exercise, you also need to use a variety of different methods to make sure you are getting well-rounded progression. My parents used age appropriateness not only to build a bond of trust, but also as a component in boundary setting. If I wanted to do something that I wasn't sure I was allowed to do, like attend elementary school dressed up as Spice Girl, for instance, I needed to check in with an adult about it. If I was able to make a compelling argument about why said thing was appropriate, then it could be negotiated. My parents were not initially aware that I would need a series of strict boundaries about dressing age appropriately in public, but it became very obvious after the third time I got sent to the principal's office for my sartorial expression. It took many negotiations and several groundings (during which I would inevitably start playing dress-up while listening to the Spice Girls) for my parents and me to find healthy compromises. I started learning about make-up and fashion design, we began talking about how to ward off unwanted attention, and we chose community events to let me safely express myself in a controlled container. As I grew older the metrics for what was age appropriate changed, and I was given more freedom to express myself how I wanted to. I had a grounded understanding of how to dress myself and what the different kinds of attention I was receiving actually meant.

Of course there were slipups, though they tended to be missed by us kids in the moment, instead being explained to us later during family get-togethers. The most infamous slipup, which gets more airtime at our family events than any other, is the time the adults of our extended polycule were piled into the living room to nail down the logistics for our "Poly Pagan Summer School." This was their answer to the question "What are we going to do with more than a half dozen seven- to twelve-year-old, high-energy, intelligent youth for the summer when most of us still have to work?" The answer was to have the parents who were not currently working full time spend their days with the children doing academia in the morning and extracurriculars in the afternoon. School was ending soon, and they needed to sort out the final details. They had done all of the logistics, scheduled a time to meet and were unsuccessfully letting the children occupy themselves; they needed ten uninterrupted minutes to be adults, and we couldn't give them more than five at a time without asking for something.

Meanwhile, I was then hosting more than half a dozen high-energy, intelligent kids in my messy room. The air was thick with hormones and body odor, and we were getting restless. I was fearful of what damage might be done to my room if I didn't get everyone's attention, and so I looked to my brother. We shared one of our nearly telepathic moments where I volun-told him he was about to become a sacrifice for the greater good, and he took a deep and heavy sigh of resignation. I pulled out a jump rope and said, "How much of this rope do you all think it would take to cover Royce's entire body?" Five minutes later, he was successfully wrapped from neck to ankles with enough left over for me to hold as a leash as we unsteadily guided his hobbled form down the hall. As we spilled into the living room like the release of a clown car, we succumbed to our giggles, completely forgetting that in our family when a child wanted to enter a conversation they stood and listened for a break in speech to say "excuse me" and would then be acknowledged. I tried to regain enough composure to show off my brother, as many of the adults suppressed giggles of their own, looking from me to my primary parents, who were slowly shaking their heads. In the midst of the chaos, my frustrated Momma Phoebe closed her eyes and without looking at us kids said loudly, "Will you just take your tie-up games *back to the bedroom!*"

We kids heard the definitive edge in her voice that sent us bolting back towards my room, toppling Royce over and half dragging him out of the room. Once out of sight, we heard a chorus of uproarious laughter from the living room. Though confused and intrigued, we didn't want to incur any parental wrath and stayed in my room until they were done. The adults had caught every nuance of Momma Phoebe's unintended double entendre, but we children truly didn't understand what was so funny about the moment. As the story has continued to be told over the years, it has become quite obvious, and when I began learning shibari rope work, my Momma Phoebe declared smugly, "Well, we always knew you enjoyed tying people up. You started practicing on your brother when you were nine years old!"

Teaching Boundaries

Boundaries were an important concept to impart, on all sides. Between parent and child, yes, but also between children and between the parents themselves. During a lengthy phone call to my bio-mother, Angi, one of the many I made during the writing process, I asked her to tell me one of the most potent things she learned about polyamorous parenting throughout my upbringing. She responded, "You know, it's that not everyone will have the same ideas about child rearing, you have to let go of control and let the bio-parent make the final decision in regard to their biological child. It gave us a way to agree to disagree."

I hadn't heard this from her before and had to inquire further. "What kinds of things did you find you disagreed about?" I heard her hesitation, even over the phone. "If you are open to sharing," I added hastily. I didn't know how deep she wanted to go on this today; consent is subtler when it's with your parents but is still a respectful consideration.

She replied, "No, it's fine, I'm just thinking. The biggest one between Jean and me was about testing and treating you for ADHD. She was convinced that you exhibited all of the symptoms, and I disagreed. Ultimately, I saw the struggle both of your siblings had with their diagnoses and medications, and I chose not to go down that road with you."

As she took a deep breath, I said, "Thank you for sharing that, Momma; I definitely joke nowadays that I'm not ADHD because I was never tested, so people can't prove anything!" We shared a chuckle to break the heaviness of the moment. I continued my inquiry with a final question. "What happened when you and Gary, who were both bio-parents, disagreed?"

"We did our best to compromise," she responded. "Your father and I had very different ideas about how to raise you religiously, and when you were a baby he was still identifying very much as a Christian, whereas I was beginning to get serious about my Paganism. He was the reason you were not raised Pagan from birth. Instead, we compromised, and you were taken to Christian church on Sundays with your father and went to Pagan church with Jean, the kids and me every full moon. You got to see how each religion was practiced and followed what felt best for you."

I couldn't help but smile at this. I remembered even from a young age knowing that I enjoyed Pagan ritual a lot more than Christian service. At Pagan church, I got to run around a bonfire once a month while people drummed, danced and sang; what high-energy young kid wouldn't like that? It may have also helped that the place the Pagan church was held had a pool.

"The only time I defied your father's wishes," Angi continued, which helped me pull myself back into the conversation, "was when you were in sixth grade, and I decided to pull you out of school and start homeschooling. He wasn't living with us at the time and wasn't seeing you deteriorating every day from the bullying you were going through. He was convinced there was another way, but I knew what I needed to do. Jean had already offered to help me set up a curriculum and have you study with Royce and Reed. I remember saying, 'I don't care what he does, I know this is right.'" She sniffled quietly, and I could tell she was probably tearing up.

"And it was, Momma. Thank you for being that brave. I know it was best for me in the long run. I honestly don't think I would've made it otherwise," I reassured her. We had been through this conversation before; it had taken my father several years to believe that homeschooling was the best option for me to finish my primary education, but my mother was right. For my safety, health and sanity, taking me out of public school was what needed to be done.

This conversation with my bio-mother opened my eyes to some of the discussions my parents were having among themselves that we kids were not privy to. I went on to ask her why they had chosen to make these decisions away from the children, and she said, "It would have been confusing to you kids! You would have undoubtedly seen it as unfair if you got to have different boundaries than your siblings. We weren't a set of best friends or aunties and uncles; we were presenting ourselves to you kids as a united family. We had to be on the same page." In this moment, I was more fully able to understand where she was coming from; they had given us kids the respect of presenting a united front and giving us structure that we could rely on, trusting that when it came to rules and boundaries, what one of our parents said was true for all of them. There was no discrepancy between the parents and therefore no room for division. This united front was a boundary our parents were using not only to give us structure, but also to give themselves some space to more gracefully figure out the difficult and complex points of their polyamorous parenting.

To their credit, it seemed that for every situation that arose, my family had set up multiple social dynamics (consensual systems for behavior), which they opportunistically used for strategic parenting. The focus for my parents was on how to raise well-adjusted, inquisitive children who knew how to draw upon the resources at hand to get their needs met. Healthy boundary setting was a key part of dealing with the constant boundary-pushing nature of children as well as curbing the appetite of us knowledge-thirsty Tiny Humans by teaching us when and how to strike out on our own to find the information we needed.

By the time I was four years old, Angi and I had the dynamic of "three why's." If she could not answer my line of questioning to my satisfaction after three inquiries of "But Momma, why?" then I needed to go elsewhere to find the answer. It was about that time when, after my third "why," I began to ask "But Momma, how come?" Sometimes she would answer me and other times she would just curse at me under her breath about how difficult it was trying to satiate a smart child's thirst for knowledge.

In any case, the information we kids received was always delivered using the lenses of age appropriateness and transparency as guidelines. Therefore, when our parents instituted boundaries, we were given the logic and rhetoric about why the boundary was being put in place. This proved to be especially important when it was a boundary that dealt with the power differential between parent and child and the children were not necessarily pleased about the outcome. Many a time, however, the boundaries for adults and children were the same. They were expressed differently, perhaps, but they held the same base concept, allowing the children to see the similarities between ourselves and the parents in dealing with our basic needs, such as alone time, dealing with emotional overwhelm, habit building and expression of our sexuality.

This brings me to the question on everyone's mind. What is said question? Sex, of course; how did my parents keep us children away from their sexual exploits, how did we not get over-sexualized at a young age, when did we lose our virginity? This more than anything else is the query that lingers on the dry lips of an eager inquirer, afraid to be asked but burning their brain cells with the anticipation of it. In my experience, when the question doesn't come out in a moment of sheer bravery on the part of the inquirer, it comes out in one of two ways:

1. When I finally decide to be gracious and put on my hat as their Own Personal Fountain of Knowledge.
2. In a salty moment of frustration where I unabashedly state the obviousness of the answer.

The former happens most often when I am getting paid for my expertise, and the latter comes out when I should be getting compensated and am not.

Due to the frequency with which I get asked this question, I have many answers to it, and there will be more answers as I go on. But for now I will let you in on how simple it can be to instill boundaries and how parents can create the personal space they need to be healthy adults, without traumatizing their children. Lucky you!

The brilliance of the age-appropriate dynamic was in its simplicity: parents got to have sleepovers with their friends and lovers, just as the children did. They negotiated and scheduled with the other parents about their dates, and when it worked out that another parent could take a child for the night, they would, leaving the parent with the date free to have their adult time. When this wasn't possible, or the children's sleepover happened to be at the house of the parent with the date, information was frontloaded to the children about the parents' expectations of their behavior. Children had a lights-out time, they slept, preferably, in a different part of the house than the parents, and they were told when it was okay to wake the parents up in the morning by knocking on the door. This was barring any middle-of-the-night emergencies or nightmares, which obviously took precedence. Knocking on the door was an egalitarian dynamic the parents held with the children. When a child closed the door to their room, parents would knock before entering, and the same was asked in return. When a child received punishment for hiding things from their parents, one aspect of that punishment might be the inability to close your door for a certain period of time except to change your clothes.

One morning after a particularly epic tribe gathering, the kids were sleeping over at a tribe mate's house where Jean and two of her lovers had had a sleepover date of their own. They were having a naked snuggle session in the morning, and it was running later than the time they had told us we could wake them up for breakfast. We were bored, hungry and feeling mischievous; thus, five children all under the age of eleven burst through the bedroom door declaring, "Nobody expects the snuggling inquisition!" and began bludgeoning the adults with questions until we stopped short, finally registering how many adults were in the bed at the time. Our eyes scanned across the bed, seeing adults, not our parents, who we were not used to seeing snuggling our mom! I remember counting them like monkeys in the bed: *1,2,3...1,2,3...wait, 1,2,3?* My mother Jean, being the intuitive genius that she is, cut us off before our line of questioning could shift to the details of what the parents had been getting up to during their sleepover.

She clearly and calmly asked, "Excuse me, why didn't you kids knock?" Our eyes widened, our breath caught in our chests and the wind flew out of our sails. We knew we shouldn't have burst into the room.

"Are we in trouble?" somebody asked Jean.

She responded, "Not yet. Go back into the hall, count to ten, knock and wait for an answer."

We stood there, half nodding.

"Now," Jean insisted, and we scampered!

Once outside of the room, we caught our breath. The kids who weren't directly Jean's children started laughing and were poked in the ribs by those of us who were. You didn't defy one of our moms, for fear of the dreaded and mythical Mommy Orge, the aspect of maternal rage and disappointment that meant you had well and truly screwed up and should be prepared to receive the consequences or else "become a set of tent stakes," as was one of Mommy Ogre's favorite metaphors for grounding.

After a slow count of ten, we gave each other the silent look a bunch of young adventurers do when about to embark into a cave of the unknown...I knocked with a shaky fist, rattling the door in its frame. In return I received a strong, clear "Come in," and I tenuously opened the door. Our nervous little faces poked around the door to find all three of the adults, clothed in PJs, open-armed and ready for morning snuggles. Upon seeing the coast was clear, we kids launched ourselves into the bed, giggling. We were met with playful tickling, cuddles and an offer of pancakes for breakfast.

In this story, my mother Jean did something very clever at the moment of surprise. She didn't focus on the sensationalist reaction *"We were caught in a moment of intimacy!"* Instead, she focused on the dynamic our family had set up about knocking on doors. She wasn't ashamed of her actions, and she didn't make a big deal out of the casual nudity and associate it with "being caught." She used a form of redirection to get our adolescent attention onto what truly mattered in that moment: a breach of boundaries. When we were in the hall, we knew there was something big we had just walked in on but were far more focused on the boundary cross, which we could potentially get in trouble for.

In this way she cemented the lesson: it's not about the sex, it's about respect and relationships. We kids hadn't been respectful, and that's what mattered. To this day, I still call out, "Hey Momma, it's me," gently knock on the doorframe and receive the response of "Hey, kidlet" before entering Jean's room, which ironically commonly has the door thrown wide open.

Adulting, Part Four: Spreading My Wings

Spring had sprung, it was my twenty-third year breathing on the planet, I had been out of my father's house for two years and living out of my car for the past thirteen months. I was operating under the assumption that I was going to make all of my sex education dreams come true as a sole proprietor, teaching independently on the road using my social network as my audience. In certain ways I was proving to be successful in my goals; early in my travels I held a successful crowdfunding campaign, raising six thousand dollars as start-up money. Some of this money was specifically set aside to attend the first year of Reid Mihalko's Sex Geek Summer Camp, a week-long business intensive for sex-positive professionals. I was using the rest of the money to support myself financially as I traveled and taught a couple of two-hour workshops for local communities across Washington, Oregon, California and western Canada. My workshops had low attendance, and I was feeling the strain of traveling so much without the payoff I had expected. I didn't recognize it at the time, but I was running myself at a pace I couldn't sustain and was doing so without a real foundation underneath me. I had nowhere to truly rest my head that didn't rely on other people, my three multiyear relationships had spectacularly fallen apart due to stress and distance, my mailing address was Gary's house, and I didn't have a backup product or offer to push at any of my classes.

Through the training I received at Sex Geek Summer Camp, I learned that I was making two major business mistakes. First, I was expending all of my energy trying to impart my value as an educator as the lowest price point via my one-shot classes. Without any material for my audience to go deeper with, they had no way to continue to build trust with me and purchase higher-ticket products. I needed courses, intensives, coaching packages or a blog; I needed to build a consistent message that would be able to reach broader audiences. Not broadening my audience was my second mistake; by consistently using the networks I already had access to, I was preaching to the choir. I was receiving support from my tribe as I always had, but my tribe wasn't the audience who truly needed my help. I needed to move away from the support I had always known and branch out into the overculture to find the prospective polyamorous, sex-positive and kinky people who need guidance and permission to explore these sides of themselves. The irony was that though I had flown the physical nest of my parents' homes, I wasn't ready to truly spread my wings and find my own forest yet. I was afraid and, without much external stimulus because I spent most of my time alone in a vehicle, I was playing out the negative tropes I had been raised with.

Don't trust the overculture!
Money is difficult to attain.

People have a hard time understanding you.
You will have to fight for people's respect.
These thoughts ran through my head on endless repeat while I was alone in my dark vehicle, hiding behind tinted windows and blasting '90s pop-punk as I gallivanted up and down the string of West Coast cities along the corridor of Interstate 5. I continued to push myself harder and harder while stewing in the thought that I didn't have enough credit to be considered a valid resource for people. Simultaneously, I was sliding into a deep depression while I was trying harder than ever to follow my dreams.

By the end of the summer and a string of increasingly unsuccessful attempts at reaching other sex-positive networks across the country, I had identified enough of these compounding issues and made two definitive decisions. One, I was going to move back home to Seattle. Being on the road had proved too difficult. I hadn't found a way to sustain myself and truly build up my business to where it could pay me dividends. Two, I was going to get a tattoo, using money I didn't really have, to mark the time period I was on the road and the lessons I learned therein. The tattoo was to be of an interrobang, the amalgamation of a question mark and an exclamation point. I felt like it was not only how Muppets end all of their sentences but also a representation of myself as a punctuation mark. To this day, "WHAAT?" and "WHYYY?" are the questions I ask most often, of both the universe and those I communicate with regularly.

I placed the mark on my inside of my right forearm, facing upright towards myself so I would have a reminder of its lesson every time I held a book in my arms. The moment the mark was embedded in my skin, I began to feel confidence in my decisions. I was going to go home, use my social capital to regroup and build my business within the security of my supportive tribe. My internal monologue had shifted, I was now able to comfort myself, saying, *It's okay, everything is going to work out in Seattle. You are making a valid and reasonable choice and others will see that.*

I used this sentiment as a mantra for myself as I packed my belongings up into my car for what I hoped would be the last time and made my way north towards the last rays of sunshine that grace Seattle in the early fall.

5

"What Does the Rest of Your Family Think?"

"You've seen relationships that are committed regardless of whether the adults are sexual with each other or not, and when that aspect of those relationships changes, you know you can let people do what they want or need to do, and they will still love you."–Jean

Coming Out

I'm continuously grateful that my family was out to me throughout my entire childhood, and I am a fierce advocate for nonmonogamous parents to be out with their children. At its essence, being out is about authentic relating; adolescents are vastly more observant than we give them credit for, reading you all of the time. They will pick up on the fact that something is going on with you and begin to build their own narrative about it. I have multiple people in my life who were raised without the knowledge that their parents were actually nonmonogamous. They have all spoken about feeling as though their parents were lying to them and cheating on each other, and how this secretive behavior made them feel unsafe and distrustful of their parents. "I just thought my mom was a slut, I couldn't respect her, and I wasn't able to see her as someone to put my trust in." With this in mind, ask yourself the following question: Would you rather:

1. Have an ongoing dialogue that may be uncomfortable at times?
2. Eventually have to have a big reveal, which may or may not be in your control?
3. Keep a secret from your child or family, about a deep and intimate part of your identity for the rest of your life?

Did you choose 1? I know I would. Is it scary to think about talking to your family about who and how you love and share intimacy? Yes, absolutely; but it's also a way to foster support for yourself and your decisions. I have always known that my family members are going to support me in my weirdness, even when they don't fully understand all that my weirdness entails. We have a history of being open with each other that has never faltered, and therefore I can trust in it; knowing my parents are weirdos with integrity who don't lie to me is a part of how my psyche developed and is a huge part of the reason we have been able to maintain emotional intimacy with each other throughout the trials of my growing up. Parents, if you have the blessing of being out with your children from the moment they are born, this means that there is never a time when they will know otherwise.

Specifically for the parents, if you figure out your nonmonogamy sometime after your child's birth, find your words, set up a positive circumstance (I do not recommend it be in a crowded place where they are not able to leave if they need to, like a restaurant), tell them as soon as you feel confident in explaining your circumstance and relationship(s), and answer all of the questions humans have when they first hear about nonmonogamy: "Do you love all of them equally?" "What about Mom / Dad / your primary partner?" "What about jealousy?"

I also encourage you to be prepared for a less-than-enthusiastic response; your child is processing a lot of information about someone who is not themself and whom they may have never thought about having intimate needs. Also, depending on how old your child is, they may not have yet realized humans have romantic / sexual needs, and this may be an unintentional precursor to the birds and the bees discussion. Prepare for reactions such as "Ew, gross!" "Why would you do that?" "How could you?" "What are *your* parents going to think?" "I'll never be able to have my friends over again!" "I don't want to meet any of your partners, ever." While these responses may pierce your heart with a flaming spike and make you question all of your life decisions up until this moment, remember that youth react directly from their emotions, and this is their form of processing. It may in time subside, but for now it is important to hear them out and honor their feelings. Remind them that they have full say in how much or how little they want to know about your partners, and that this doesn't mean they have to be out about their parents being this way, but that you didn't want to hide from them *because* you respect them. Continue to breathe and comfort your child in the way that you two connect the best.

I do encourage you to be prepared for the worst, as an option, but do not dwell on it to the point of manifesting the response. This is the twenty-first century, and it's likely your child has access to YouTube, Tumblr, Reddit and the other corners of the internet where nonmonogamy is a commonplace subject. If not the internet, there is the good old peer-fed rumor mill, which I can guarantee has burned through one or two hints about people's parents "being open...like swingers!" Your kid may not have a strong reaction at all, which could feel depressingly anticlimactic. I recommend seeing this as an opportunity to relish how far our society has come and start setting up the dynamic of "If you have any questions at all, know that I am always open to talk about them with you." This gives them the opportunity to come back to you, one question at a time. Alternatively, they may be your biggest advocate to the rest of the world in ways that you will never see. Kids are enigmatic like that, and it's part of what makes them great!

No matter how a child reacts to this, you are engaging with them in an open and honest way that is modeling for them how to come to you with strange or difficult topics in their life.

At this point, your mind may be coming up with a bunch of circumstances that prevent you from coming out to your family, which I understand. This also begs another question: How many of these reasons are circumstantial, based on external factors? Your day job, your conservative extended family, your custody situation, the unwelcoming nature of the place you currently live; these are all valid reasons not to be out to everyone you meet.

I'm not encouraging you to be reckless; keep yourself and your family safe, first and foremost. However, I suggest that you can be out to your family without being out to the rest of the world. This does involve creating boundaries with children about how you discuss your family outside of the house, which we'll cover more in the section "Living with Two Faces." You can set up your home and family as a safe haven to fully be yourselves and teach the children in your life how to choose how to present themselves in different company. Don't keep information from your children because you feel it might be too much for them. Instead, set boundaries around how children receive information so they are able to process it in an age-appropriate manner. You do this by being upfront and including them in setting boundaries for the family, giving them access to knowledge and therefore empowering them to choose who to safely share the personal details of their life with, and how. Reciprocally, when space is created where children can always count on being heard and understood for who they are, it gives reprieve when navigating the larger world. From my experience, I can tell you this balanced approach helped me develop skills around tactful social engagement and emotional resilience from a young age, which helped keep my family safe and together when facing a world that actively looked to distrust us for being who we are.

Outing Others

I need to take a moment to acknowledge that there are numerous ways of "being out." They are not on a continuum, and you are encouraged to engage with them in the ways that are most comfortable for you. Coming out is an ongoing process that you will participate in for the rest of your life, and every time you do so will be different. It is also prudent that I let you know: it will not always be your decision to come out. There is always the possibility of being outed by circumstance or miscommunication, and you will need to figure out how to react, process this, and move forward in a way that makes the most sense for you, your family and your current situation. I wish you luck with this; being outed is a process that takes resilience and courage of a kind that you may not believe you possess right now. I believe you will find your strength and do what is needed, as I did.

———————

When it came time for me to finally inform Angi about my inability to be heterosexual, I was shaking with fear, stumbling over myself trying to find the right words to tell her I was attracted not only to boys, but also girls, queers, trans people, gendernauts and, honestly, most anyone who could hold a stimulating conversation. I was trying to find the words to tell her I had always felt this way and most importantly that I had been keeping this information from her for a long time because I was scared of her judgment. This fear was unfounded. I shouldn't have feared her judgment; she has always been relentlessly supportive of me. Instead, what I received was her condescending smugness, which in the moment felt worse.

Angi smiled widely and said, "Oh, Mousey. I know that. You have talked about feeling this way since you were little and only stopped when you started getting bullied at school for it. I suspected you were going to turn out this way and I have to say, I'm glad you are exploring this now. There's less chance of you getting pregnant!" Thrumming with shock, I steadied myself; I took a deep breath in, searching for the relief I desperately desired from this conversation as Angi continued, "Besides, your Auntie Louise told me a year ago after reading about it on your LiveJournal."

My breath caught in my chest, my relief polluted with rage. *She's known the entire time and hasn't given me any clues! Doesn't she know I'm going through hell at school, that the bullying hasn't stopped and I'm throwing up most of my meals due to stress? Is she even paying attention? Doesn't she see how unhappy I am? She thinks she knows ALL about my sexuality, she doesn't know anything!*

And how DARE Louise, she obviously doesn't have any respect for me and the sanctity of my journal. I don't care if it's publicly online, Angi specifically stays away from it so I can have my space to vent. Louise knows this and decided she knew better! That's the last time I'm sharing anything with her.

I could not figure out who I was more upset with, Angi or Louise. I just stood there, dumbfounded as my mother hugged me in celebration.

Each human is unique. We each have specific experiences and traumas that influence how we come out and to whom. I was not afraid of coming out to my tribe; I chose to do so in a forum I knew most of my community had direct access to. What I was afraid of was hurting Angi and falling short of any expectations she held for me. I was a confused teenager trying to figure out how to trust my bio-mother and her ability to accept a complex identity that meant I was not likely to provide her the classic parental hallmarks such as watching her child get married and having grandchildren. I was using the safe space that I had carved for myself online to process these things before talking to Angi about them. A space that Louise had been an active part of maintaining, or so I had thought.

Throughout my life, Auntie Louise had been a safe person for me express myself with; as Momma Phoebe's sister, Louise was a tribe member who was close to our family unit. She was the cool auntie, and I trusted her to understand the sanctity of my privacy. Through these actions, however, Louise had betrayed my trust in a big way. Despite my content warnings online about the information on my journal not being shared with my parents, when I confronted Louise on the topic, years later, apparently she thought I had already talked to Angi about my sexual orientation and thought she hadn't needed to confirm this with me because I had already put it out online, for the world to see. Through her assumptions, she had outed me and broken my trust in a way that wasn't able to be repaired for years to come.

At the time, I was furious that such an important part of my life felt out of my control and needed somewhere to place my anger. My rage fell upon Louise. She was no longer my cool auntie, but someone I needed to keep at a certain distance and to never again entrust with information I wasn't ready to be public. It is difficult for me to divulge that my attitude towards her has persisted in this fashion for a long time, and until the writing of this book, I was actually unable to be transparent with Louise about this. I had been acting in a way that kept me safe from her betrayal, protecting an old hurt for my confused teenage self. Eventually, as I was sifting through my memories and putting them on the page, I realized I was being unfair to Louise by not telling her about my feelings. When I actually engaged her in conversation about it, she apologized immediately, owning up to her mistake and saying, "Seems like you had every right to be upset with me. I betrayed your trust. My hope is that in the future you feel comfortable enough to come to me with your feelings, even in conflict." Proving to me once again that family are the people most willing to engage with you, through it all.

———————————

Your relationships with your friends, family, coworkers, doctor and any children each have their own particular dynamics, and while you may find it easy to come out to your friends, the idea of coming out to your family, your coworkers or to the general public might be difficult enough that the action becomes debilitating. It's okay to take your time coming out; treat yourself with kindness, and don't be ashamed if you feel like you need to compromise how to present your authentic self to the rest of the world. We each make compromises to live amicably within the bounds of society, and it is not necessary for you to be out to every single person in your life, especially in circumstances where your safety or livelihood is at stake.

My encouragement for your coming out comes from a place of understanding that everyone has extenuating circumstances in their lives that may prevent them from being out due to the need for self-preservation. I hold no judgment about this; my family developed a full system for coming out to those outside of our local alternative community.

Living with Two Faces

By now, it may seem as though my childhood was all giant gatherings full of peace, love and harmony. Don't get me wrong, there was a good amount of such time spent in community. But these gatherings were so prevalent because we needed community, as we all were living with various masks in the nine-to-five portions of our lives. Living as an out polyamorous family is not a simple experience for any of the members. My family has always operated with a healthy sense of paranoia regarding the access people had to our family, and there was a gradient in how much you got to see. We traded access for trust; "Child Protective Services (CPS)" was considered a curse word in my house growing up and was only spoken of in hushed whispers with serious faces. CPS had no intention of understanding us and had demonstrated it was not our friend.

As a child, I primarily experienced this gradient through the act of having friends over to my house. It was an act of coming out and required skills akin to those you need for a high-stakes act of espionage. It was our mission, should we choose to accept it, to be the successful and unashamed example of nonmonogamy at my school. It was a mission that took delicacy, negotiation and occasionally misdirection.

Phase one often consisted of me visiting my school friend's house several times before the topic of coming to my house would ever come up. Before the invitation was extended, I needed to figure out the answers to some basic questions:

- How much detail does the school friend have about our family?
- How open-minded are the child's parents?
- How many hoops will we have to jump through to explain ourselves in a way that is safe and makes sense to them?
- Would my mom have to put her shirt on?

My parents' paranoia was instilled in me from a young age, and I knew that once the friend was invited over, they had access to a lot of information about who we were and how we functioned. Sometimes it was safer for us to simply be the "eccentric hippie family" as far as my school was concerned. I did grow up feeling somewhat two-faced, unable to be my fully authentic self in the outside world, and it was a bit unnerving to know from a very young age that the society I lived in wasn't entirely safe. At the time, it was weird, but the more I look back on it I have come to realize this experience helped me exercise resiliency and gave me perspective about what stressors were truly important. I don't feel fragile about the state of the world because I've always known it's a complex and not always friendly place.

Phase two would commence only if the friend reacted well to my blunt, adolescent explanation of what my house was like: "It's super fun! I have a huge yard, an old siege elephant I use like a treehouse, my dad lives in the basement and his girlfriends come over to visit once a week. My mom is upstairs and sometimes my other mom comes over with my brother and sister, who are also my cousins. Oh, and we have a dog!" If this engagement was deemed successful, I could bring the request to my parents. Once my parents had worked out logistics regarding the other family and what level of knowledge the fellow child was capable of handling, I was allowed to extend the invitation.

Phase three was a crucial time. The friend would come over, and everyone at the house was made aware that we needed to be on our best behavior. We didn't need to act like a repressed, nuclear family; we knew that wasn't believable. We needed to be the version of ourselves that was similar to what we showed the media: friendly, grounded, congenial and in many ways "just like you!" This was not the time to showcase the age-appropriate casual nudity, open discussions of sexuality and endless humor at the expense of the overculture that was commonplace in our everyday life.

Upon completion of phase three, it was a waiting game. The school friend would go home and regale their parents with a blunt, adolescent explanation of what they saw: "There were a bunch of adults who were dating each other, and they have a hot tub that you can't have swimsuits in! We didn't go in it, but Koe's moms were telling me swimsuits are bad for the water. So, why do we wear swimsuits when we go to the pool? Are our swimsuits bad for the pool water? Oh, and they have a dog!" And the parents would react however they saw fit. The ball was out of our court, and no matter how much we made light of people being able to "handle us weirdos," there was always an underlying tension about us needing to be prepared for the worst possible outcome.

Phase four was maximum security, only for those friends who had proven they were able to handle everything our family had to share. They often held similar beliefs to my family and either had open-minded parents themselves or, as in one special case, lied through their sweet, blessed teeth to their overbearing, conservative mother to come hang out with us. These were the ones who reached the level of Best Friend, who ended up spending a lot of time at our house and Angi inevitably would end up colloquially "adopting" as her nonbiological children. In some cases, I was "adopted" reciprocally by their parents as the artistic, wild-spirited family friend.

I have been told multiple times over the years that though these friends didn't necessarily understand all of the working dynamics of my family, they are grateful to have had the perspective of a nonmonogamous family when they were growing up to help them accept the evolution of sexuality, gender and relationships we are experiencing in the early twenty-first century. For all of the risk we were put in, we never had a serious run in with CPS, and I am glad my existence was helpful to these friends.

In the Media

For the life of me, I could not get comfortable. I was sweating inside clothes that weren't mine and could not shake the feeling that something intense was going to happen. The feeling wasn't coming from the hundreds of eyes on me or the pressure of being on national television—that part excited my performative self. It was how forced everything was. The stage lights were hot and overwhelming as I sat on the stark white couch, so firm and uninviting. During the commercial break, I had I nervously tripped over my words while trying to express my appreciation, telling Tyra Banks how much I wanted to be like her when I get older, and she responded with a rehearsed "Awww, thank you so much" as she sweetly patted my hand. She was nice enough with her thousand-watt smile and gentle demeanor, but her hand was bony, and I could tell her focus was on the other million details demanding her attention and not on my awkward compliment. She was so very put-together: perfect makeup, large wavy hair and well-pressed clothes. I had been following her since I was a child. I admired her power as a curvy woman of color in the modeling industry and I dreamt of one day being a contestant on *America's Next Top Model*. She was one of the first idols I ever had, and perhaps that was why I had jumped at the chance to represent polyamorous families on her new talk show.

My father Gary, his long-distance partner Dawn and I had recently appeared on *The Montel Williams Show*, and our poly-cule was on a roll in the media! Tyra's show had contacted us not long after Montel's; they seemed like they were trying to be respectful...to a point. Enough to not make us lose our shit but also nosey enough to make good television, and the contract reflected this sentiment. Angi, Gary and I had been flown to Los Angeles, where we were going to be on the show with Dawn, her husband and their girlfriend, as well as six other guests. Even with more guests than necessary, the show was interested in highlighting me as the child of a polyamorous family. A crew had come to film our polycule in Seattle at the home Angi and I were living in with the quad she was involved with at the time.

The experience of filming had been a whirlwind thus far but was going fairly well. The show had gone all-out to make us feel well represented; they dressed us very chic and negotiated every question with us to make sure they were asking it in a respectful manner. Once on stage, we filmed all of the segments in the order they would appear in the episode. Dawn's interview had focused on the triad's internal relationship dynamics and hadn't gone into Dawn's twenty-five-year relationship with Gary. During our interview it had come out that Angi and Gary hadn't been romantic for a few years at that point, and we began discussing their other partners. Angi spoke of her live-in quad (Storm, Angi, Gina and Eugene), which cued the video we shot in Seattle depicting our extended polycule, including Gary, his current wife, Jules, and the couple they were both dating. They were a folksy husband and wife duo Gary had known for more than a decade, and he was still somewhat dumbfounded at actually getting to date them. After the video ended, Tyra looked at Gary and, going off-script, asked him, "So, are you bisexual?" To which my delightfully blunt father answered, "Yes."

I felt my surprise well up. I tried to quell it in front of the cameras, but this was big; my dad had just come out on national television! My parents and I had discussed sexuality at length over the past couple of years as I had delved into the LGBTQ community, but I had been so wrapped up in my own experience I really hadn't given much thought to my bio-parents' identities. Angi and I continually debated her sexuality as she continued to define herself as eighty percent straight and twenty percent bisexual, which broke my brain *(Doesn't that mean you like women ten percent of the time?)*, but, as she often reminded me, she had accepted my sexuality, and I needed to accept that this identity was true for her. Gary, on the other hand, was going through a pretty significant sexual journey with his kink identity. Through his kink, he was opening himself to engaging with men in a variety of different ways, and it was apparently affecting how he viewed his sexuality. I knew he had been dating both members of the folksy, outwardly heterosexual couple, and I had seen them all be affectionate with one another at our household functions. But I had mostly seen this behavior as another connection in the larger polycule and honestly hadn't put two and two together until he had definitively spoken his truth to Tyra—and her entire viewing audience.

I was more proud of him than I had words for, which was probably for the best because I was wearing a microphone, and as far as the cameras knew, I was completely aware that my father was proudly bisexual. I saw it on Tyra's face; she knew she would not be able to debunk this sentiment. The clear and confident way he had presented his answer let it be known that his declaration would not be trifled with; his energy was radiant and electric. This was a property I had seen my father's pride take many times, and it was an energy to be reckoned with. To Tyra's credit, she recognized this and redirected the conversation on to our next negotiated talking point.

After we heard from a couple looking for a hot bi babe of their own and listened to a few dissenting opinions about nonmonogamy, the final segment was one where they brought back the guests "of interest" to let the audience ask them questions. I was once again sitting on the unbelievably firm white couch along with two other guests, awaiting the onslaught of unnegotiated questions. Once Tyra was situated in the crowd aside the first inquirer, the cameras began to roll. The inquirer was female-presenting, somewhere in her mid-twenties, with a mischievous smile gracing her face. "Yeah, so my question is for Koe. I just wanted to know if you're still a virgin?" I swear the entire audience simultaneously stopped breathing, all of their eyes were fixed on me. I peripherally saw the other guests on the couch silently sending me their support; they knew just how invasive that question must be to a sixteen-year-old femme staring into a television camera.

The following is a catalogued list all of the reactions I was having to the question:

1. What the eff? *How dare you!* Are *you* still a virgin?
2. My virginity literally has nothing to do with my being raised polyamorous! I see what you are doing and, whether intentional or not, the question you are actually asking is: Does raising children in a polyamorous family turn them into teenage sluts?

3. Which definition of sex we are going with? I mean, does getting fingered by my girlfriend count? (Fun fact: my girlfriend later told me she thought it had counted as sex and I had lied about my answer on the show. That was not a fun conversation.)

4. Why does this matter?

I wish I could tell you that I had these thoughts clearly laid out in the moment and that I spoke to them as eloquently and fiercely as I wanted to. In honesty, these responses have only become clear to me in retrospect, over the hundreds of times I have replayed this moment in my head, trying to figure out how one person could so blatantly disrespect my privacy over something that was obviously intended to create drama. Actions like this are pure sensationalism, and I knew I wasn't going to allow myself to fall into its trap, but I didn't know how to respond. The clearest feeling I had in that moment was the sensation of a release valve opening for all of the stress and nervousness I had been experiencing during the show's production process, and I was ready to get bold. I held the fresh memory of my father's declaration ringing in my head and responded, "Yes, I am."

I'm not sure which was more unnerving, the blasé expression the young woman wore as she sat down or Tyra's condescending reaction to my answer. She raised her eyebrows, softened her voice and overemphasized her words, "You *are* a virgin?" I reaffirmed the answer I had given her in the same proud-to-the-point-of-defiant way that my father had, and the audience gave a me significant round of applause. They were indicating that they were proud of me, because they assumed I had been able to stave off of sexuality amid this culture of adult promiscuity. Tyra played into the audience's assumption by continuing her questioning with, "And, you're waiting for marriage, or...?"

This time I had my answer well and ready. "I don't know if I'm ever going to get married. I just haven't found a person I want to be *that* connected to yet." At that point, Tyra moved on to another audience member's question, and I took a calming breath. On the post-filming car ride to the airport, I reflected on how well I had actually done with the question: I had been brutally honest without being snide. I held my composure and gave an informed answer that the audience praised me for, even if they didn't fully understand or agree with my statement about not having a specific intention to get married. I really was honing my skills at responding to the media and was taking a sense of pride in it. I was doing the work in the media for those who didn't have the ability to be out in that fashion.

Being out in the media has some very particular stressors associated with it, and I understand why many nonmonogamous and sex-positive people choose not to become a mistreated side-show attraction in the media circus. I have found that my acting background, giant support network and sheer shamelessness has given me a certain comfort interacting with those who are looking to make my life into something that will boost their ratings. When we had finally wrapped the Tyra Banks episode and it was in post-production waiting to air, I was touting the affair as a positive media experience. Though it was indeed sensational (it's daytime television after all), the show had treated us with respect, did their best to take the subject seriously and made sure to outweigh the negative perspectives on the show with the positive ones.

On the night our polyamorous tribe gathered to watch the episode together, I felt proud of the work we had done. Everyone gathered in the theater, which was coincidentally the same room the film crew had shot us in months before. Everyone was booing at the right moments and cheering on my mother, father and me for our bravery. It felt like we had really made something that could provide reassurance to the people out there who had no tribe and were desperately searching for a term to describe their desires. We were a part of a piece of polyamorous media that had good representation, good editing and was well received. Sounds too good to be true, doesn't it? Turns out, it was.

The evening after the show had aired, Storm, who was a member of Angi's polycule and the primary breadwinner of our household, came home with his signature pep stolen from his step. He asked all of us to come together for an impromptu house meeting and informed us that earlier that day his boss had asked him to come in for an unscheduled meeting to discuss something. Storm was a premier psychiatrist for Seattle Mental Health, in a management position, and though he did not advertise his romantic life at work, he was the head of the national Unitarian Universalists for Polyamory Awareness group, and he never outright hid his identity. During the requested meeting, Storm's boss proceeded to inform Storm that an email had been forwarded to him that said Storm had recently been involved in what the boss described as "a despicable piece of media which is inappropriate for someone in your professional standing."

During this meeting, the boss demoted Storm from his position in management purely on the grounds that Storm had participated in this media piece. The demotion included a pay cut and affected his reputation with the organization. At this juncture, I need to make two things very clear. One, Storm did not come to Los Angeles with us; he had been filmed only in the segment we had shot in Seattle. Storm, being a caring and conscientious man, had been considerate of his involvement in the media piece. His image was distinct in only one ten-second shot in which each member of the tribe came to huddle around the couch in the theater, one by one, to indicate the breadth of connection within our extended network–style polycule. He had no quotes and no depictions of public displays of affection in the entire segment. Two, Storm had participated in other polyamorous media pieces in the past where he held a larger role, including full interviews. But these pieces of media were on a much smaller production scale and weren't as likely to be seen by people who felt offended enough to send an email like the one his boss had received.

This situation was a targeted act of discrimination against Storm, and we, as his family, wanted to know who had done it. Someone who knew Storm directly had specifically gone out of their way to send this email. Our assumption was that it was a coworker with an unknown grudge, but we could never be certain; the boss didn't give away any information about who had sent him the email, because he didn't have to. Polyamory currently has no legal protection in regard to bureaucratic discrimination and can therefore be used against anyone based on the narrative the accuser has built around their assumptions of nonmonogamy. This reality is, understandably, a prime reason for many people to not be out about their nonmonogamy, particularly when it has the capacity to directly affect their family.

I do not advocate coming out if you feel as though you could risk destabilizing a foundational part of your life: safety first. I do adamantly recommend having clarity about what being out could mean for you, good, bad and ugly, and having contingencies for what happens if that choice is taken out of your hands. The harsh truth is that at some point, in some way, large or small, you will be outed, and it will have ripples that you cannot control. These ripples might be fantastic! They might be harrowing. No matter what happens, you will still have control over how to react to them, always. I recommend this so strongly because Angi's cross-quad didn't have any such communal fore-thought and each built their own narrative about whose fault it was that this happened and internalized the experience in a way that ended up breeding resentment throughout the house. The situation went as far as being a keystone argument during the course of the polycule's break up.

A distinct motivation for my writing this book is to provide guidance to other families based on the mistakes that were made in mine. I truly hope you are able to take these lessons to heart and build a successful structure from them, for yourself and your family! If you end up being out in some fashion in your life, whatever that looks like, I urge you to recognize that your bravery is someone else's representation of what's possible. The more people who are able to be out, the more others can see the breadth of what nonmonogamy looks like and may even ignite the ember that some have banked in their own chest, waiting to light.

Adulting, Part Five: You Can't Go Home Again

Winter had come to Seattle. I couldn't get grounded, and it was becoming increasingly unbearable to be in my car all of the time. The skies were dark and heavy with storm clouds and the dank must of the "Pacific North-Wet" winter had moved into my lungs, causing an exhausting chest infection that was on its second month of habitation and seemed to have no intention of paying me any rent. I couldn't breathe without heaving, the dark circles under my eyes were trying to take over the world and I could not find housing for the life of me. I found several couch surfing situations that kept me out of my car for the most part, but every permanent housing option I inquired about through my network had found a way to fall through for negligible reasons. There was no drama or ill feelings; I was just receiving a genuine Seattle freeze in a way I had never experienced before.

I have always had an anthropomorphized relationship with the place I live, seeing the city-wide dynamics as personality traits and engaging with my residency as a form of intimate communication between myself and my partner of sorts. During this time, I was angry with Seattle. It felt as though she had lost all of her love for me. She wasn't providing for me in the way I had come to expect, and I wasn't being a good partner in return. I was trapped by my own insecurity around poverty; I believed that I couldn't get a well-paying job and wasn't good roommate material because I was "too weird" to deal with, an old insult from childhood rearing its ugly head. I was desperate to find something that would help me ground and center myself. I was a native Seattleite; didn't that mean I was automatically deserving of a quality life within her? Turns out, gentrification doesn't work that way.

Internally, it would take me years to realize I basing my expectations off of receiving, but I wasn't giving during this time. I had fully expected to come home into the loving arms of my tribe and that everything would be okay. I expected things to be as they were before: to receive financial help, have opportunities handed to me, and lean on the abundant emotional support of partners and family! I had yet to discover in my adult life that when you leave a situation, things move on without you, and you can never truly go back to a circumstance just as it had been. My communication with Seattle was coming from a place of resentment, and she was responding in kind.

Externally, I wasn't able to recognize the large-scale shift Seattle was undergoing at the time. The extensive gentrification of Seattle's metroplex through technological boom and real estate buy-ups was staggering; everyone was in a state of needing to focus on survival and self. People simply had less bandwidth for creating community with others, and I didn't have enough of a foundation to stand on to be valuable to those around me, specifically in regard to homesteading. It's not that my tribe didn't love having me around once again or want me to succeed in my housing and stability goals; it's that they didn't have capacity.

I know it was incredibly difficult for my bio-parents to be unable to provide for their child in this way; Gary had to fill his house with renters to help cover the mortgage, and Angi was stuck waiting on approval for social disability benefits and living off of subsidies. It was a time full of tearful hugs from Angi and lengthy conversations with Gary about logistics for converting a portion of his garage into a small studio apartment. Jean, Jim and Reed were all going to college and living in a home that was already too small for the three of them to study properly. Phoebe was living alone in Las Vegas, where she had moved to find steady teaching work. And Royce was in a similar situation to mine, couch surfing and trying to keep a job.

Though it was an undeniably bleak time for the family, we continued to watch out for one another in the ways we knew how to do best. Whenever there was excess from what someone received from a subsidy or the food bank, we would share it with one another. When someone's car broke down, we would give each other rides to needed appointments. We made sure to regularly check in with one another. We were a family, for good and ill, in harrowing times as well as abundant ones. I could see everyone's hardship, but I was still unable to shake this harbored resentment at them for my woes. If we could have just been a bit more "normal" (more like the overculture), then I would have the tools I needed to succeed, even if the tools were ones that didn't align with my ethics or integrity. I was blaming my feeling stuck on my family, still seeing myself as a byproduct of their influence.

By the time New Year's Eve came, things had turned slightly in my favor, but I was still weary and deeply concerned about the shoe I felt dangling above my head, ready to drop. I had negotiated a three-month sublet with some very gracious friends, my longest-standing partner and I had gotten back together, and I was working enough that I was able to abate my panic and experience moments of calm, however fleeting they were. I was by no means settled, but I was finally receiving support and gaining more understanding about why the past six months had been so difficult for me. I was making good use of the developing prefrontal cortex that was coming online as I transitioned from my early twenties into more solidified adulthood.

I recognized that since getting my interrobang tattoo, I had been having a major growth spurt. I had been taking in new information at an unprecedented rate and hadn't been able to find mental stability on which to base the rest of my decisions. I found the ironic symbolism of this exceptionally humorous: interrobangs are all about asking questions emphatically, and I had oriented the mark inward, directing the questions towards myself. I was twenty-four, my frontal lobe was actualizing, and I couldn't get my life together, perhaps because it just wasn't the time and place for me to do so. I was trying to live out old patterns when new variables had changed the playing field. I needed new input and new strategies to take on the new lessons that were undoubtedly coming. I'd been clinging to the cocoon that had once kept me comfortable and now seemed to be stifling my opportunities for further growth. The idea of breaking out of my old patterns was terrifying, and I didn't know what I needed to do to actually shed my metaphoric chrysalis. But I was now fully aware that Seattle, my beloved hometown, was giving me the boot.

I was reluctantly understanding that I wasn't going to be able to make my dreams come true in Seattle because it wasn't actually the place I was meant to be. There are lessons that you can learn only by leaving your hometown and experiencing somewhere new. The time had come for me to get crystal clear about my tangible goals, my base needs and how much I was willing to compromise to achieve them.

The first piece was fairly obvious to me. I thought that staying in the United States was a reasonable decision and have always known I am a West Coast kid. I reflect at the ocean, the wild weather mimics my wild spirit and there is nothing more grounding for me than spending an afternoon hiking through a forest of evergreens. Second, I knew I wanted to continue doing sex education and preferred a culture that valued the arts, sex positivity, kink and political progressivism. I desired a place with recognizable ethnic diversity, something Seattle's institutions and culture are very good at glossing over and not giving voice to. I knew these desires were steering me towards an urban environment rather than a smaller rural community, which would also support my goals of business networking and having access to travel, if needed. My daydreams were becoming more and more clear about where I wanted to go next, but my outlined parameters left me with a limited number of options. San Francisco was the one that intrigued and terrified me the most among them, but I wasn't allowing myself to see it as a viable option, mostly due to the insecurities around money and imposter syndrome that had been holding me back all of my life.

I had been curious about San Francisco since I was a preteen watching *Charmed* and romanticizing the Summer of Love. Currently, my brain was playing an aggressive game of ping-pong with itself about the subject: *Why stick to the West Coast? There are plenty of other places that are culturally different and farther away from the place I grew up!* This logic is undeniable, but I was still experiencing a deep sense of wanderlust and needed somewhere engaging enough that it would demand I spend my energy settling into it versus constantly dreaming about the next horizon. San Francisco has the combination of mild coastal weather and a constant, bustling culture in conjunction with the ever-present anxiety about the cost of living. San Francisco was the most expensive and infamously complicated city in the United States to live in at the time, but every time I imagined strolling through Haight-Ashbury, my internal go-getter disposition was aroused at the very thought. I was also nervous to stray too far from my home and family in case of any emergencies. In California, I would be in the same time zone, at the edge of my beloved Pacific Ocean and in the middle of one of the most powerful city centers in the world.

The move itself would require I challenge the idea that I wouldn't be able to make enough money to make it work. I would need to heighten my situational awareness in order to keep myself safe, living as a solo, femme-presenting person, and I would need to put my bureaucratic life together enough to be self-sustaining in the face of California's convoluted legal system. Everything seemed to fit my needs, goals and desires in just the ways I needed them to, but I hadn't yet been able to even look myself in the mirror and speak my truth aloud. My parents' fear of straying too far from the known was hanging over me like a dark cloud, and their voices were whispering inside my head the same question that every person currently living in the Bay Area was already asking themselves: *How would I be able to afford it?*

The answer to my subconscious question of the universe regarding my desire to move to San Francisco came in the form of a roundabout adventure in the middle of the Pacific Ocean. An adventure that resulted from an off-hand joke I made with my father on a dark and rainy December evening. I was standing in the outrageously decorated '60s kitchen in the house Gary had inherited from his mother when she passed. I was leaning against the avocado-colored oven insert, warming my hands with a mug of steeping peppermint tea and listening to Gary talk about his plans for his next trip to Maui, Hawai'i, with his fiancée, Rose. After Gary had split with his first wife, Jules, he had found a local kink community on Maui and taken a lover there. He was undeniably besotted with the island and is the type of person to truly nerd out about the things that intrigue him. Maui being a place rich with history, botany, geology and marine life, he was over the moon. Gary had been scuba certified multiple times throughout my childhood and had recently begun to share the experience with Rose. The two had frequented most of the underwater parks in the cold, murky Northwest and were yearning for a bright, colorful landscape to explore. Rose had just sold her house to move in with Gary and was treating the two of them to a scuba-heavy vacation on Maui. I could only chuckle at their childlike enthusiasm; the sparkling blue light that shone in my father's eyes when he talked about the crystalline waters of Hawai'i was mesmerizing, and I completely understood why Rose had decided to create the opportunity for them to have this adventure together.

As happy for them as I was, when I stood there warming myself against the oven and nodding along with my father's excited explanation of how the Hawai'ian islands are technically the largest single volcano directly connected to the ocean floor, I felt myself begin to flush with jealousy. Gary had traveled to

Maui twice, had already taken a girlfriend who he'd subsequently broken up with and was about to go a third time with his fiancée. Throughout all of the sharing Gary did about how much he thought I would love it, the subject of a father-daughter trip to the island hadn't come up at all.

My family has had a tenuous relationship with disposable income, but when it was at our disposal, we spent money on adventure. I have always thought of my parents as a band of Lost Boys and Girls; though they learned how to be functional adults, they made sure to never lose their sense of childlike wonder and mischief, and they fiercely protected us kids from the parts of the world that sought to destroy those parts of us too. Gary and Angi specifically valued life experiences, and there were many times we told my school's administration we had a "family affair" that needed me pulled out of class. When I began homeschooling in junior high, my curriculum was built to support the things I was already actively engaged in, and as long as I maintained balance in my educational pursuits, the sentiment often repeated to me was "This is your life to live, and there are experiences that you will not find in a classroom. Take advantage of the opportunities you will never be able to recreate."

As I stood there, I realized how much I wanted to go with him and Rose to explore somewhere I had never been. It was an overwhelming sense of understanding, and I knew in that moment it was profoundly important that I get myself to that island. I did something I learned directly from my father: I used my wit to make a bold and potentially inappropriate statement. As he was finishing his sentence "...I am so excited to take another of my girls to Hawai'i," I responded, "You know, there's one of your girls you haven't taken to Hawai'i yet." I hid my face behind my tea mug as I said it, but I cocked my eyebrow and compulsively flipped my hair to emphasize my point. No matter how many times we've had the pronoun conversation, I have always remained my father's "little girl" and in that moment, I decided to use it to my full advantage. He stared at me for a heartbeat longer than I was comfortable with, and I started to sweat. *Oh shit, did I go too far and offend him? He's helped me so much in the past few years as I've been trying to get on my feet, and I know how expensive a trip to Hawai'i would be.*

As my anxiety flared, Gary cracked his winning smile and said, "You want to go to Maui? Oh honey, that's wonderful! I bet you Rose would be happy to get you a ticket to the island, and the folks we are staying with often host people from the community. You could even teach a class and then it would be an educational trip for you, so you can write off most of your expenses. You know, if you want to, we'd have to push it, but we can also get you certified to go diving!" I sighed in relief, sending a whoosh of steam up my nose from my closely held tea mug. *Of course he would try and figure out a way for me to teach to the local community. He has always been my biggest fan. Oh, I should stop him though; he's going to get the tape measure for my wetsuit, and I don't have an interest in scuba!*

We would be on Maui for two weeks at the beginning of April. As March came around, I began to lean into the idea of not being in Seattle, of shedding my layers, putting the rest of my possessions in storage and taking the upcoming months as they came. I was still unsure about making the move to the Bay Area; I didn't want to force it if it wasn't right but instead used one of the strengths I picked up from my parents, trusting my intuition and treating myself like a fully capable being. The more I leaned into this thought process, the more I was able to breathe and face each day with resilience and compassion. Seattle seemed to be responding in return, and the weather was turning from its endless torrent of rain to the meteorological smorgasbord of early spring. *It's a wonder anyone who lives in the Pacific Northwest is able to maintain a solid mental state with weather like this. I can't wait to be on a beach, basking in sunshine.* Thoughts of warm sandy beaches carried me through my remaining weeks in Seattle before the trip, and on the eve of our departure, I was able to finally lull myself to sleep with the thought *At least I'll have a couple weeks of respite and not have to worry about figuring everything out just yet.* Little did I know how many things I wasn't expecting about this trip that would end up causing me joy and surprise. Starting with the fact that though Maui has many warm sandy beaches, it also has frequent rainstorms and subsequently produces more rainbows per capita than any other state in the nation!

The day had come. It was a blustery April morning when Gary, Rose and I piled into an airport shuttle, made our flight out, and five hours later landed on the island, all with relative ease. The moment we stepped out of the heavily air-conditioned airport terminal, the heat hit us like a wave, warming me all the way to my bones and informing me I had worn far too many clothes, as they were now sweatily sticking to me. I peeled them off, blinking into the bright Maui morning. The sun was illuminating everything with a deep saturation of color. The sky was electric blue, the grass a rich, glossy green, and I could tell that if I was not careful I would have a sunburn within minutes.

We three had all done a fantastic job of communicating throughout the hectic travel logistics but began to break down a bit around the time we were working on getting our rental car and figuring out where to get food. Even as we settled into our first night at a hotel, I could tell I was feeling off, not jet lagged or upset, just ungrounded. I couldn't find my bearings, which way was north or my connection to the earth. Having always lived on the mainland, even residing at the edge of the ocean, I was used to the feeling of a huge expanse of earth and cardinal directions that I was able to tap into when I needed to calm myself down. The same is not true for an island: the land is directly in tandem with the water, the ocean holds you up and feeds you. Maui itself is a pair of circular land masses with an isthmus connecting them. The island exists at a slanted angle that cuts diagonally across the longitude and latitude lines of the earth. It was a completely new style of directional relatability for me and, as though I were flirting with a new person, I was trying to learn the island's communication style before assuming an anthropomorphic relationship with it.

By the next afternoon, as we arrived at the house we were to spend the rest of our visit at, I was so nauseous I was ready to pass out. I felt as though everything was spinning and Maui, the trickster himself, was laughing at me. I shared an anguished look with Rose and understood that I wasn't the only one having issues with their energy levels. Rose was a devout, powerful Wiccan priestess with numerous magical credentials, and she couldn't figure out how to ground either! Gary had been so excited to be back and show "his girls" his favorite island that he hadn't quite caught on to how ungrounded we both were. When we got out of the car, we immediately went to each other, dropped to our knees and began to pray. My faith has always taught me that no matter what, the earth is beneath you; even in the middle of ocean, deep, deep down, you are always connected to mother earth, and she is able to hold you to her. Thanks, gravity!

I said this out loud to Rose, and we took a long breath together. We must've looked like a solid pair of hippies to our hosts, a couple of haoles (a Hawai'ian word meaning "white and/or nonlocal person") on all fours in the grass, breathing rhythmically. After Gary had greeted our hosts, he turned, having noticed we hadn't joined him, and came over to ask what was wrong. We explained as best we could, and he put a hand on each of our backs.

"Do you remember what I told you about Maui, Koe?" My father has always had a knack for using moments of comfort as opportunities to impart knowledge and wisdom.

"Which part?" I asked. "There have been so many things you've told me about this island."

He chuckled gently. "The Hawai'ian islands are one of the largest direct connections to the center of the earth! What you are kneeling upon is lava rock. There are no layers of sediment in between you and the bedrock; it's bubbled all the way up from the mantle to the surface, coming to meet you! You want to feel grounded and connected to the earth? You are touching some of the closest source material you will ever get access to."

Gary has always been exquisite at a poetic one-liner, and in this case he was also correct; even if the energy of the islands moves differently than the mainland, up was still up, down was still down and mother earth was holding me. I felt Rose shiver next to me, and I held her hand as Gary scooped us both up into a giant bear hug and whispered to us, "I am so excited to share this place with you two, my favorite girls."

Once he let us go, we all went over to meet our gracious hosts. They were a triad who were about as kinky as you can get, and though they were far less spiritual than we were, they joked, "Hey Koe, Maui nearly shook you off the island, didn't he? Had to see if you could handle paradise!"

6

"Aren't You Being a Bit Greedy?"

"You had a variety of role models and learned multiple interaction styles, in a trusting, openly communicating environment. This set a standard for how to treat people that you all have taken into your general interactions with everyone you encounter." –Phoebe

Adulting, Part Six: With Both Feet

My first week in Maui passed in blissful ease. We spent equal time exploring numerous beaches, parks and tourist destinations and time with our hosts discussing kink, philosophy and island life. Gary and Rose had connected with a local dive shop that had great deals on tours, and they were itching to take me out with them. I agreed but hadn't gotten any diving certifications and would be one of the few snorkelers in the group. We set sail on the seventh day of our trip.

The first destination of our tour was Molokini, a huge dormant volcano whose ridge extends up from the surface of the ocean and leaves a glorious basin in its submerged crater for coral, fish and other marine life to gather in. I hadn't worn snorkel gear in a decade, and as I flopped around like an uncoordinated waterfowl, I noticed how nervous I was to be trying something new and how much I was resisting the experience. I was alone, staring down at one of the most intricately textured landscapes I'd ever seen. Due to my vantage point, one hundred and fifty feet above the crater's floor, everything looked white-washed and barren, as though someone had bleached all of the coral. I learned later that this was due to how light diffuses into water, and if I had gone down with the scuba divers, I would have seen a riotous landscape of color.

I knew that going through the rigmarole of getting certified wasn't something I had capacity for before the trip, and as I was already having enough of a challenge with snorkeling, I honestly could not have handled scuba at that point. I was taking this adventure at my own pace, continuing to listen to my intuition, and as I began to get a handle on moving with the fins, I paddled out to the submerged edge of the crater, where the boats gained entrance to the protected cove. Out here the reef grew up and over the wall of the submerged crater and clung to the outside wall of the volcano; here I was approximately twenty feet above the reef and was able to see everything with vastly more definition.

From this vantage point, I could see the wonderful complexity of coral and fish who were brave enough to venture out to the edge of their safe cove; but my body's newly formed self-preservation instinct also became very aware that I was swimming along a precipice and that on the other side of this ridge was a sheer drop down into the depths of the open ocean. I was on the edge of safety, staring out at the great unknown, and it felt like a huge moment of metaphor for my life. Here I was, finally free of the web I had been clinging to in Seattle; I was halfway across the world's largest ocean in a place I did not know and engaging with a culture that I was doing my utmost to respect while clearly being an outsider. I was also taking the time to rest and be fully in the moment versus constantly worrying about how I was going to survive each and every upcoming challenge in my life. I felt no barriers between myself and all the opportunities I desired, a decidedly new feeling for me, having come from a poverty mindset. I felt as if everything was possible from here, and though I didn't have solidity about what my next move was, for once I wasn't worried about it! I treaded water, staring into the unbelievably aquamarine abyss and battling my own agoraphobia until a wave from the cove bumped me over the edge of the crater into the open sea, as though the ocean herself had heard my thoughts and was urging me forward, saying, "You want the horizon, go get it!" I shrieked through my snorkel and scrambled back over the rim of the volcano to the safety of the cove. I may have been a haole tourist but knew enough to not get too cocky with the ocean; she always wins.

Back on the boat and zooming off to Turtle Town, our final destination, I was approached by one of the two humans on the trip who were my age. I initially classified him as another surf-bro hipster who was looking to get into some self-centric conversation. But when he introduced himself with "Hey, I'm Mike, how are you doing on this beautiful day?" I saw something in him that caused me to toss away my preconceptions. He spoke of things with such a gratitude for life and excitement for each moment, it was easy to be charmed by his exuberant presence. When we arrived at our next destination and the divers were getting their gear ready, he invited me to jump off the port-side railing of the boat's upper deck and into the open ocean with him. I furrowed my brow at him in response. Smiling, he said, "It's cool, I got permission from the captain." I looked over his shoulder to confirm, and the captain was waving at us to come above deck. Once we were clinging to the outside railing, we looked at each other, and I felt it, the undeniable spark of chemistry—or maybe it was just the endorphins talking, since we were directly in the middle of an adventure and all. He looked at me, his face shining with excitement, and he said, "On three..." I nodded, and as we jumped, I felt all of the apprehension about the deep open water release; the ocean wasn't pushing me into danger, she was encouraging me to delve even deeper into the feeling of freedom. I basked in the water as long as the captain would let me, until he told me to come back aboard and I could do it all over again!

After we had been flinging ourselves into the open water for a while, Mike decided to forgo diving this leg, instead joining me. We grabbed our snorkel gear and headed out to go explore the terrain. Most everybody on the island had questioned me about not getting scuba certified, saying that I was missing out and would have a moment where I wished I had done it. I had been fairly resentful of this sentiment and hadn't seen anything that had made me rethink my decision until Turtle Town, with its layers of caverns teeming with marine life and schools of fish shimmering through the water all around you. I became increasingly aware that I was only getting a bird's-eye view and the only way to get more of the experience I wanted was to literally go deeper. I took a huge breath of air and submerged myself.

I have been swimming my entire life and have great confidence in my ability to navigate water safely, but free diving turned out to be a whole different kind of challenge. The currents were strong, the fauna was distracting and the pressure on my eardrums intensified the more I pushed towards the things I wanted to see. I kept running out of air before getting close enough to explore something closely and would have to fight my way to the surface to rest and oxygenate. Mike came up to me and asked if I was okay. I told him I was having a hard time keeping up with everything I wanted, and he asked me why I was pushing so hard, why didn't I just relax and enjoy the experience for what it is? I told him, "It's just so beautiful, I want to go scare fish and look for turtles. Who knows when I'll get to do this again?" I felt like I was on fire; I wasn't truly angry that I couldn't dive the way I wanted to, but I was over-stimulated enough that I wanted everything at once and wasn't focusing well.

Mike seemed to be able to read my emotional state with disturbing accuracy and said, "I've lived here a long time and have practice free diving. Tell me what you want to do, and I can scare the fish and show you where the turtles are?" He was so astonishingly earnest in his offer, I accepted. As we swam along, I pointed at clusters of fish and he jettisoned himself towards them, causing the fish to scatter in every direction! I got so much delight from seeing them explode away from each other like a living firework and seeing Mike's self-satisfied smile as he returned to the surface, to me.

We had swum more than a thousand yards away from the rest of our group, and when Mike said we should begin heading back to the boat before it left us, I agreed. As we turned to swim back towards the boat, I spotted a sea turtle gliding resolutely in our direction, barely five feet under the surface of the water. I had received many warnings that sea turtles are endangered and that it is against state law to touch them; in Hawai'i sea turtles have the right of way. We're the ones invading their habitat after all. In awe of seeing such a graceful creature, I froze; I was uncertain about what to do, and the sea turtle seemed to have zero intention of changing its course. I looked to Mike for some guidance, but his gaze was directed downward, and there was concern on his face.

I followed his gaze and found what was so concerning; another sea turtle, twice the size of the one ahead of us, was pelting straight upwards in a direct collision course with where we were floating. I needed no prior knowledge of sea turtle behavior to recognize the kind of body language that says, "Get the fuck out of my way!" We had to go, now. Mike and I looked at each other and instantly developed a nonverbal plan. We turned back around and swam as fast as we could, creating an awkward arc to avoid the smaller sea turtle. As we sprinted out of the way of the adult turtle and back towards the boat, we kept a close watch on the two turtles, who had found one another and continued to swim in the same direction as we did, twenty yards beneath us. We didn't seem to be on their radar anymore but were not going to let our guard down, just in case we were wrong.

Once we had safely pulled ourselves onto the deck, I collapsed, dramatically gasping for breath and clutching a stitch in my side. Mike came and clapped me on the shoulder. "You did good back there, another minute and we would've been dragged away by that honu, never heard from again!" he teased.

All I could do was glare at him as I regained my breath. Once I had stripped out of my wetsuit and stuffed calories in my face, I realized I didn't fully understand what Mike had said. I went to the Captain and asked, "What does 'honu' mean?"

He gave me the overly patient smile most locals on the island had when I said or did something that particularly showcased how much of a haole I was. "Ah, it's the native Hawai'ian word for turtle." I nodded humbly and explained the encounter Mike and I had had with the two turtles as we were returning to the boat.

The captain laughed outright and said, "Sounds like you and my boy had what we call a *honu experience*." He said this in such a strained fashion that I knew he was making a truly terrible pun.

After sharing an appreciative groan, I asked him, "What do you mean by 'your boy'?"

The captain chuckled again as he shook his head. "He didn't mention it? Mike is my son. He honestly hasn't been out on my boat for a couple of years, but lucky for you he decided today was the day. He is a good one, I'll tell you that. I hope you two have fun." He gave me an egregiously cliché smile and wink. In turn, I stood there, classically dumbfounded; I guess I now knew why it was so easy for Mike to get the captain's permission to jump off the side of his boat.

Once back on dry land, Mike came to say goodbye, wished me a relaxing trip on the island and began to walk away. Gary, Rose and I were starting the engine of our rental when Gary informed me that he thought someone was trying to get my attention out the window. I turned my head and saw Mike's shiny, weather-beaten face practically pressed against the glass, waving at me. Once I'd recovered from jumping out of my skin, I rolled down the window to Mike snickering. "Sorry about that. I just wanted to provide you with this, if you would like to get together and see a more local side of the island." He handed me his phone number, scrawled on a damp piece of paper and waved as he headed back to his buddy. I looked up from the number to Gary and Rose grinning devilishly at me from the front seat.

"Well, he seems *nice*," Rose said.

I was still a little too caught off guard to come up with a snappy response and instead just blushed and put my head in my hands. "It honestly wasn't my intention to pick anyone up in the middle of the ocean while breathing through a rubber tube!" I exclaimed, and the whole car burst into a fit of laughter.

Of course I called him; wouldn't you? He was deep, witty, intelligent and wanted to show me around. I was intrigued by the offer and honestly needed a bit of breathing room from Gary and Rose. Like good hippies, we met up at the Earth Day festival happening in town and ended up spending the rest of the day together. He took me around his neighborhood of Kīhei on the back of his scooter, and then we got dinner. We ended up back at his place, and I didn't go home to my hosts' house that night.

Our connection was electric. I felt so comfortable with him, like I had known him for years. We didn't agree on everything or even have a full understanding of each other, but we were both eager to learn and shared a mutual respect for perspectives different than our own. We spent every day together, and he found time within his work schedule to join me on many of my remaining adventures with Gary, Rose and my hosts, all of whom enjoyed his presence and how adorable we were together. It was coming up on the end of my second week on the island, and I had spent more than half of my remaining time with him. The NRE had come on very strong and we were a bit drunk on each other; we had begun saying that we loved each other, and we were both dreading my leaving the island.

One particularly gorgeous morning, two days before I was set to leave for the mainland, I was making us breakfast, and he came up behind me, wrapping his arms around my waist and nuzzling my neck. "I don't want you to go," he whispered into my hair.

I shivered at his words and leaned into him. "I know, I don't want to leave either. Honestly, I'm unsure what's left for me to go back to…" This thought had been on my mind during the last several days of the trip; I had wrapped up all of my loose ends in Seattle in preparation for coming to Maui. I had no house, my belongings were in storage, I didn't have a job to go back for, and my one remaining partner and I had been drifting apart over the past six months.

I had never before in my life considered Seattle to be anything less than my home, my grounding and safety net, but after spending a fortnight on the island, I was gaining some insight into why my winter had been relentlessly difficult. Seattle had been making it clear to me that she needed a break, and I was not going to learn what I needed to by staying with her. She had broken up with me when I went to live in my car; she was not going to take me back, and it was time for me to move on.

Mike pulled me closer into him, cradling me into the press of his warm body and holding me fast with his immensely strong arms; being a hard-core landscaper, he had impeccable arms. "Why don't you just stay for a while to figure things out?" He squeezed me subconsciously during his inquiry; he wanted me so much it thrummed through his entire body as he touched me.

I closed my eyes and tried to ground myself; it was so hard to keep my wits about me when I was near him, huffing his pheromones and getting drunk off of his eye contact. "Because," I responded as I pulled myself out of the embrace to turn around and look at him, "I cannot live out the trope of being the white haole girl who finds a local boy, falls madly in love and moves to the island on a whim."

We had been having this ongoing dialogue, and Mike did not enjoy hearing this perspective. "Is that all you see this as? Am I just another part of your exotic vacation experience, an attraction to check off of your list?" His question was full of spite, pain was etched on his face and it was heartbreaking to witness.

"No, of course not," I reassured him. "It's the opposite. You're a wonderful person with a rich life, and I'm surprised by how strong our connection is. I wasn't expecting to connect with anyone on this trip, let alone someone I could fall for. You've been such a blessing for me." I looked fully into his eyes and showed him my sincerity as transparently as I could. He still looked upset as I went on, "I am so unbelievably happy here with you it's surreal, like I'm high on something." He raised his eyebrows at me. "Besides the weed!" I exclaimed. He laughed at that. "I'm trying to think like I'm in the middle of a really good high; is what I'm experiencing because I'm truly this happy, or is it because what I took was top-notch stuff? I'm not saying I don't want to stay; I am beyond tempted. I was so unhappy during this last year that coming here and meeting you feels overwhelmingly relieving, but I don't want to build something off of this 'high' feeling if there's no foundation to support it. That's not respectful to you or the island."

His expression had shifted; he was listening actively now, and I could see the gears starting to turn in his mind. He was plotting something. I continued, "If I were to move to Maui after being here for two weeks, to be with someone I only just started seeing, who my partner hasn't even heard of yet...it's an incredibly rash decision that I don't feel comfortable with, even while riding my high. Does this make sense?" The twinkle had returned to his eyes; I could tell he was about to reveal his plot.

"I don't want you to make a move you don't truly want and definitely don't want you to make any major decisions purely on my account. You're in charge of your life and your happiness, always. I can also tell you never slow down; ever since you've been here, you've run around doing all of the touristy things you can fit into your schedule! That's not what island life is really about, though. It's about taking your time and appreciating every moment of your day as much as you can. I keep hearing you say that you're happy here, and I think it's because you're finally starting to relax a little bit. When I said I wanted to show you the local perspective, I didn't just mean the bar down the street; I want to provide you some space to relax and think about what you want to do next. I'm not asking you to move in with me, I just want you to slow down for a second!" I simply stared at his smug smile; he seemed to have a way of cutting through the mental mazes I put myself in and provide me the kind of honest perspective I needed to hear in the moment.

I still wasn't convinced, though; *how much time are we talking about?* He read my mind and said, "How about another two weeks? You can finish out the month here and move on to whatever you feel like doing next, after you've had some time to rest. I will even buy you a new plane ticket back to Seattle so you don't have to worry about the cost. How does that sound?" I bit my quivering lip and looked anywhere but at his face. How can you honestly turn down a beautiful person you are smitten with who's offering you two more weeks in paradise? I was shy in my response, nodding my head in his general direction. He responded, goading me, "I learned recently that I shouldn't move forward with you unless I get an enthusiastic verbal yes. What am I supposed to do with a noncommittal head nod?"

His wit caught me off guard, and I playfully stuck my tongue out at him. "Yes, that sounds wonderful, thank you." I pulled him in close, and we shared a lingering kiss that only built in its intensity...He was late for work that morning.

Adulting, Part Seven: Facing Fears

The night before my original flight out, I told Gary and Rose that I wasn't going with them, that Mike had invited me to stay with him and I was taking him up on it. They were thrilled and jealous; they would have stayed too if they didn't have obligations to get back to. Gary handed me an extra hundred dollars spending money and made me promise to keep in contact with him so he could make sure I was okay. Two hours after Gary and Rose landed back on the mainland, I got a call from my wonderfully dramatic mother Angi, jokingly demanding to know, "Who is this boy who has stolen my baby away to the island, and do I need to mount up a rescue?" I reassured her that Gary had met him, and he was a fine, upstanding gentleman.

She appreciated me saying such and asked in a more serious tone, "So, you've known him for a week, and you are in love with him. Do you think you might have a wee bit of NRE going on, Mousey?" I responded that I was very clear on the fact that I was deeply in NRE and that's why I wasn't staying forever, just for another couple of weeks. She asked, "Do you have a plan for when you get home? I moved all of your stuff to the storage unit, it's all tucked away." I told her I didn't but that I would inform her when I had a plan. We said goodnight. I grabbed my pipe and a blanket and stepped outside to think.

The night sky was majestic; the moon was waning gibbous, and the stars were out in full force. On a clear night in Maui, you can literally see all the way to the other end of the galaxy. There is so little light pollution that you don't just see the haze of the Milky Way in the sky. You see the definitive arm of the other side of the galaxy arching high above your head, informing you that no matter how much humans like the idea, we are not actually the center of the universe. I cast my eyes down as my agoraphobia flared up again, thinking about how vast the universe was and how small my issues were in comparison. I huddled into my blanket as the wind began to pick up and furrowed my eyebrows; *why have I been making things so hard for myself?*

For the last year, I had been attempting to make unmatched puzzle pieces fit together. I was in a new phase of my life but using old methods to try to cope with my problems. I needed to fully engage with this new state of being and figure out what my values were, without the familial influences I had been letting dictate me. I had witnessed most of my fellow polykids reformulate their identities in relation to their parents' influence, and it wasn't all pretty. Many of them chose to engage in much more closed forms of relationship structure, having seen the epic mistakes their parents had made and not wanting that for themselves. Closed relationships are totally valid, but I didn't feel that way. I found my power in the counterculture identities my parents also held; but each and every decision I made about those identities was done intentionally.

I knew I was definitely not monogamous from the moment I watched the infamous proclamation from Tom Cruise to Renée Zellweger in the film *Jerry Maguire*. I saw a shell of a human desperately begging someone else to fix him and knew with absolute certainty that I never wanted someone standing at my door, drenched and professing "You complete me!" It's not my job to complete people through codependency; I knew I would need someone who is full of life and getting their needs met through connections to other people in addition to me.

Similarly, I needed only to learn the definitions for the terms "queer" and "sex-positive" to understand they described me. As a preteen, every single session of "playing house" with my female friends included an experimentation component, and my parents had been getting calls from my school principal telling them I had been sharing "inappropriate reproductive information" with my classmates since the second grade. I was happy to share the same identity markers as my parents. My teenage rebellion hadn't looked like any other person's around me; instead of hating my parents in my teenage years, I focused on distancing myself from my maternal extended family, who were the ones I felt the most judgment from about who I was. Since I had left my adorable studio apartment and hit the road, however, I had been struggling with the feeling that my childhood hadn't actually prepared me for the big wide world, but I hadn't yet been able to put a finger on what felt so off about my childhood model.

Since my neurological development had gotten to the point that my prefrontal cortex was fully online and running its own background processes, I was gaining loads of new perspective and starting to see which identity labels I focused on and frequently pulled strength from. Queer, sex-positive and polyamorous are what help me be a badass special snowflake, but they are not the only ones that make me unique. I needed to look deeper.

"So, what's always been true about me, I mean besides being a queer, polyamorous pervert?" I spoke my thoughts out loud to the dark and ruffling wind. "Well, at my core, I am a go-getter. I have always driven myself towards the things that I want, and if there wasn't a way to attain them with the resources at hand, I manifested creative solutions to make them work. Remember last year, when I fundraised six grand in three months?"

I pushed on before my negative reactions to this thought could take over. "I am also caring. I have immense capacity to hold space for people, occasionally to my detriment. I have a knack for putting others ahead of myself." By acknowledging my capacity to sometimes let others' needs run roughshod over my own, my negative voice had quieted, and the only internal response I had was a condescending *aaaaand?*

I rolled my eyes at myself. "...And, I'm undeniably a performer, always have been. I have the relentless need to express myself and use my body as the tool to exhibit whatever concept I'm trying to portray. I have a long-standing creed for myself to be an example to others of what freedom looks like. I aim to be proud and open about the things people are curious about and afraid to live out themselves. I call myself a harbinger of freedom, for goodness' sake!" I covered my mouth as the echoes of my exclamation faded from the yard and turned my head to catch the eyes of my hosts through the window. They both wore a look on their faces that plainly said, "That is some powerful stuff Koe must be smoking." Funnily enough, I had forgotten to even light my pipe once outside.

"Always making a scene, aren't you?" I whispered under my breath, breaking their eye contact and walking deeper into the yard, continuing my conversation with myself. "It's so like you to take this offer, always running towards the adventure. This isn't a bad thing, but also remember how you've been yearning to settle down and put your roots somewhere? It's important to acknowledge that part, too." Near the edge of the property, I stumbled on a breathtaking nighttime vista, showing off the western mountains on the other side of the island. As I stopped to admire the view, I continued the line of thought in my head.

When I run towards adventure, it's not always a need for distraction. I also run because I need something to keep myself engaged. The adventure doesn't need to be travel. I have a smart and eager mind that likes to munch on complex concepts and connect them to the larger whole! I feel most content when I have something fun and purposeful to put my energy towards. As much as I want one place to rest my head and call home, I need to dig in somewhere that has enough going on to keep me engaged so I won't follow my wanderlust after a few weeks.

The words came out of my mouth before the thought was fully formed. Standing swaddled in a light blanket, staring into the shadows, I said, "I want to live in San Francisco." As soon as the words escaped my mouth, my resistance kicked into high gear and my internal narrative changed. *You haven't had a real job in two years! You have three hundred dollars to your name, most of which you received from your dad on this trip, and you want to move to the most expensive city in the country? What makes you think that's going to work?* I felt the warmth of my tears splash onto my cheeks then instantly turn cold in the wind. What was I thinking? *I'm a millennial without a college degree who isn't a technological whiz kid.* This was a decision fraught with obstacles.

I had been having this thought whisper through my mind during my entire time on the island. *What if I didn't go back to Seattle upon my return to the mainland but instead went to the Bay Area?* The desire had been blooming in me since I first visited the Bay two years before. San Francisco and Oakland have similar cultures to Seattle in their progressivism, support of the arts and booming counterculture communities; both places had also experienced violent gentrification in a way Seattle hadn't known yet. The Bay Area's attitude was more aggressively forthright and street smart and appeared to demand a sense of self-confidence I desired to learn. It also held the attraction of not being my hometown, fraught with reminders of my past mistakes and recent misfortune. I wanted to be somewhere that would teach me new lessons for my new chapter of life, and the Bay Area's reputation made it seem like it would be happy to sharpen my edges a bit.

The issue with this desire was that the Bay Area was attractive to thousands of people for similar reasons: it's beautiful and bustling with a booming economy and mild weather. In 2014, San Francisco itself was deemed the most expensive city in the United States to live in and was experiencing a monumental housing crisis; these hardships were real and were the arguments my negativity was using as fodder for my internal debate. If I hadn't been able to make my life work in a city where

I had an integrated support network, how was I going to live successfully in a city where I had only a handful of acquaintances? I didn't have an answer to that question but nevertheless felt the push to go for it, jump into the deep end and see what happened. Staring out from my swaddled chrysalis, I recognized that one of the biggest barriers holding me back was the self-limiting belief that I wouldn't be able to attain the thing I wanted because I was too alternative and larger society would not give me opportunities to prove my value.

The longer I stood there, fighting the cold instead of going inside the warm house, the more I began to get brutally honest with myself. I was continuing to think about things from a basis of fear, the same fear my parents had instilled in me from the time I was old enough to go to school and begin interacting with the world on my own. Do I think my parents had intended to instill this fear in me? No, I don't; I understand that each conversation about having a "tribe-appropriate self" and an "overculture self" was their way of teaching me how to use subtlety and omission to keep myself safe and be able to navigate society at large. Throughout my life I have learned that though parts of my identity put me in the minority, I also hold immense privilege being a white, able-bodied, educated American citizen. The identities that put me in the minority are ones I am able to navigate by omitting them when necessary. This ability to pass as "normal" is privilege in and of itself, an ability that my parents view through the lens of fear and the feelings of oppression and having to hide themselves from the larger world. The fundamental difference in our understanding of this concept was one of the first places of divergence I truly felt with my parents' perspective, and it continues to provide me with a grounded sense of how to engage with the world.

As I found myself feeling more grounded, my rational thoughts began to stir up once again. *It's not that my parents are wrong for their belief, but I don't think it's entirely true. When I open myself to being a source of confident education, people generally treat me with respect. If I don't feel safe, I don't need to engage, and that's also valid; but passing up opportunities for growth because I am afraid is letting the overculture win. I don't know if I will be able to make all of my dreams come true right away, but the Bay is a solid next step, and if it's too much, I can always go back to Seattle and start over again.*

"The only person who needs to believe I can do this is me!" I said it with gusto and felt a rush of warmth flow to my face. I was flushing with excitement. Why was I fighting this urge? Looking back, I had been subconsciously preparing for this for months, putting my belongings in storage, keeping my employment open-ended and intentionally keeping my remaining relationships at arms length. In my heart, I had been moving away from Seattle for a long time; no wonder she wasn't giving me the space I needed to thrive. I began to laugh uproariously and dance around the yard, spreading my blanket wide and spinning in circles. It was the kind of celebration you have when you finally realize how oblivious you have been to something that has been trying to make itself clear to you for a while. When the adrenaline had run its course and I was beginning to shiver, I made my way back inside.

As I entered the kitchen, my hosts gave me significant looks, confirming that they had heard all of the outbursts and laughter of my epiphany session in the yard. "Everything okay?" they asked.

I responded with a nod. "I had some thinking I needed to do, and sometimes it gets a little loud."

They nodded slowly and asked, "Did you come to any conclusions?"

"Yes, I'm going to move to San Francisco when I go back to the mainland," I stated proudly.

My hosts gave me a look I would become incredibly familiar in the coming months, a mixture of respect and disbelief. It sounded like I was trying to do the impossible; I knew it to be improbable, but I wasn't ready to believe it was out of my reach just yet.

The next day I moved my belongings to Mike's house and told him my exciting news. "You know how you said you would buy my ticket back to the mainland?" I asked.

He responded with a slow "Yeah..."

I shifted into my confident posture and said, "I don't want to go back to Seattle. I'd like to go San Francisco instead." I let the excitement show on my face.

He gave me the same look my hosts did; I could tell he did not understand why I would want such a thing, but he wasn't about to keep me from what I plainly wanted. After a minute, he shook his head and said, "Whatever will you make you happy, my dear. You find the flight you want and send me the bill."

I squealed and hugged him close, speaking softly into his ear, "I am so glad I found you, thank you for supporting me in all of the ways you have. I could not have done all of this without your encouragement." I pulled away and looked deeply into his eyes, showing him the depth of my love for him. He tugged me in for a messy kiss, and thirty minutes later we were frantically throwing our clothes back on, bickering about whose fault it was that we were running late for our afternoon plans.

The gifted two weeks passed blissfully, nothing but day-times spent on the beach and passionate evenings with Mike. It was precisely the break he had wanted for me, and I took it on without hesitation. As my time on the island was coming well and truly to a close, I began shifting my thoughts forward to how I was going to support myself once I got to the Bay. I had set up a temporary place to stay and a few good couch-surfing options after that; I was feeling confident I would find something sooner rather than later. Mike was equal parts supportive of my next adventure and judgmental of my location choice "Frisco, really?" he would say with such disdain that I had to institute a safeword when we would start to argue about it. Yes, Maui is beautiful, but I knew it was not for me in the long term. And besides, he had already bought the plane ticket.

When I left the island, Mike and I promised we would continue to converse regularly and visit each other at the soonest possible opportunity. "I'll even come and visit you in...Frisco, if that's what it takes to see you again." As I boarded the plane in Maui, I began to feel the first waves of anxiety roll over me, and by the time we hit our cruising altitude, I was wishing I had stayed in the complex comfort of the island with the first person I had fallen for in years. As we landed, however, my mind frame switched over to travel mode and I dragged my heavy suitcases to my new crash space and all of the adventures that awaited me in this new city.

7

"Are You This Way Because of Your Parents?"

*"One of the most important qualities we tried
to instill in you is staying honest with yourself,
because when we choose to live in nontraditional
ways, introspection is important."–Jean*

Adulting, Finale: Finding Stability

There are few things that bring me more joy than basking in the late summer of the Pacific Northwest, the two months where clouded drizzle gives way to glorious warmth and sunshine, illuminating the abundant evergreens that give Washington the title "the Emerald State." The waters of the Puget Sound glitter a deep cobalt blue, and the people come out of their shells more than any other time of year. I find folks are either elated from regular access to natural vitamin D or else passionate about their detestation of the weather, counting down the days until the heat abates and the clouds return. I hadn't been back since I flew off to Maui and found my path to the Bay Area, but I was returning for my ninth year of Camp Ten Trees, now having successfully transitioned from camper to counselor. I continued to attend camp to reconnect with youthful queer energy and provide both space and mentorship to the other kids with nonmonogamous families who had found their way to the camp in all of the years after Sue and I sat in my first-year cabin explaining polyamory to the rest of our cabinmates.

Attending camp was the longest-running tradition I'd had from my teenage years through adulthood, and I felt at home there in a way I felt nowhere else in the world. However, this was the first time I was coming to camp from far away, having built my life outside of my home state. I was proud of what I was building in California and excited to show my homegrown queer community what the confident, adult version of myself was. I had been residing in the Bay Area for six months. I was steadily finding day work and playing the subletting game. It had not been an entirely easy spring, trying to set down my roots; Mike and I hadn't lasted as a long-distance relationship, and I had not yet found my way to the stable home I was searching for. The lessons I had discussed with the universe about sharpening my edges were of daily relevance as I navigated the housing crisis and violent gentrification of Oakland and San Francisco.

Though I was still several months off from finding perma-nent housing and my future career in social work, there was a spirited determination I was using to manifest these goals that I had not felt since leaving my father's house to go on the road all those years before. I was creating something for myself, using not only the skills I was taught by my family but also the newfound ideology I had built for myself.

I can build my own resources.

I will get paid decently for my work.

I do not need to be there for everyone if I do not have the bandwidth to do so.

I do not need to rely on others to get my needs met.

Simultaneously, I was also learning that I am still not an island, even as a solo adult. I came to the Bay Area with a small set of community connections that were proving to be fruitful and spread further into the rest of my West Coast community than I had first imagined. I was being directed towards not only sublets and job opportunities but also networking events, play parties and a weekly potluck that reminded me strongly of the polyamorous potlucks we held at Storm's house, which had been such a fundamental part of my teenage years. Finding the potluck was one of those events that ended up being a metaphor for the much larger arc I was going through. I was delighted to be engaging in the rituals indicative of tribe, which I had missed so dearly; but now I was getting to do so with a set of people who were not only a decade closer to my age but also had no connections to my polyamorous family of origin. I could be myself, make mistakes, process my childhood and have an adequate dating pool without the constant reminder of the fact that I was doing such with people who had all known me since I was a Small.

I had found an alternative community of my very own to share day-to-day domesticity with, to work through our traumas with, to share our successes and dreams about buying land to build our own permaculture, intentional living, community venue with! Honestly, at this point in my life, I have to actively stop myself from chuckling in the face of people who gush to me about their "crazy idea" of owning land to build intentional community on, especially when they do so with the smugness of a teenager who has convinced themself they've just invented oral sex. Don't get me wrong, I love helping people realize these dreams and can't wait to have a couple dozen retreat spaces spread across the world to go and visit someday. But my brain also can't help queueing up a firmly implanted song lyric from my childhood while I relive the hundreds of hours of the same conversation I've had with the older alternative generation on the very same subject: "We're going to move to the country, with half a dozen lovers! We're going to move to the country, so honey, squeeze on over," from Gaia Consort's hippie anthem, "Move to the Country."

I felt a tug at my shirt sleeve that pulled me out of my reverie. Turns out I had been basking in a sunbeam, gazing at glowing evergreens for a moment too long. I was in the middle of two hundred staff and campers navigating an all-camp activity transition, and it was time to gather up some youth to head off to the activity I was leading, Family Mapping. I looked down at the shining face of this youth, one of the ones I returned to year after year to give all of the wisdom I had gained in the past decade. This youth had provided me such joy and fulfillment as I watched them continually reinvent themself within the contained safe space of camp, which doesn't exist for them in the outside world, and is the very space I get to help create and facilitate! This youth, so full of life and wonder, looked at me intently and asked, "Can I switch out of this activity? It was my second choice, and I want to go boating instead." The comedic irony was so perfect, I couldn't be disappointed that this kiddo didn't want to hang out. But the fact was the kid had been put in this activity for a reason and couldn't switch out willy-nilly.

I shook my head, smiling, and said, "Nope, sorry, boating is full, which is why you didn't get in. This'll be fun, I promise. I brought glitter gel pens!" The camper sighed audibly, rolling their eyes at my pompousness and kicked the dirt while I gathered the other campers and we headed out to the activity.

Ending: How to Unscrew Yourself

It took me close to thirty years to figure out that the narrative I had been hearing all of my life about people feeling like they are screwed up was incorrect. Telling yourself that you are functionally defective in some way doesn't give you the credit you deserve for the functioning you do daily, and by doing this you are giving away your autonomy, your power. Your conditioning gives you a framework with which to view the world, which you can then build your viewpoints from. But, as I did, you may have to move past some of your own conditioning along the way.

Even though I had a childhood full of support and ideologies I agree with, I had to shed a lot of the conditioning I received to find myself. I also had to do this in the larger framework of a world that isn't structurally set up for the kind of conditioning I received from my family.

The society I live in has told me that my family inherently screwed me up simply by expressing love and communication in a way that is different than the norm. It's been incredibly hard to not let that messaging influence my perspective, both of myself and my upbringing. I constantly fight my insecurity about my inability to hold a long-term partner or attain the white picket fence dream the overculture has tried to indoctrinate me with. It takes a very solid understanding of self to be able to navigate this cultural landscape, which I thankfully have due to the influence of my family's teaching. I applaud those who have to do this navigating without the fundamental background of sex-positive polyamory to guide them. It's also this sense of gratitude that has tied me to my parents and their way of thinking so fiercely, and this ferocity has occasionally caused me to remain stagnant in my process of self-discovery. I started this book by sharing a moment where I felt as though I was nothing more than a product of my upbringing. Even the name I have chosen to brand myself with, Koe Creation, is indicative of the idea that I am the culmination of my parents' collaborative efforts to create the epitome of their ideological dreams! As I mentioned, there was value in this way of thinking; it helped me develop a confidence in myself as I was learning how to be an adult in a world that largely does not have a fraction of context for who I am. It helped me survive. Eventually, though, this idea became a cage I had locked myself into, the feeling that I was destined to be solely a reflection of my parents, including their shortcomings, which were becoming ever clearer to me as I leaned into my adulthood.

For me, understanding the importance of having ideologies and opinions that differ from the ones your family holds was an essential process for me, because mine so closely resemble that of my parents. I had to move through the trope that says every family screws up their offspring to find out which aspects of my conditioning I can draw on to support me harnessing my power, instead of being victim to it. Before I learned how to do this, I let my insecurity dominate my sense of self-worth. When I became so stagnant I was asked to leave Angi's household, or when I couldn't find a way to live in Seattle anymore, these were both times I felt particularly screwed up and angrily blamed my upbringing for it. When I was able to begin asking the tough questions, of myself and my family, about the ways in which I felt traumatized and underprepared, I was able to develop my internal compass for how I was going to need to navigate this life.

So, how did I find the strength to ask these tough questions? Through a process of analysis and discovery largely supported by a psychotherapist and the elimination of daily use of marijuana from my life. I've seen marijuana's benefit for those in suffering and don't deny it, but for me marijuana was a crutch that I used to mask the hardship I felt while learning how to be an adult. I needed enough grounding to find out which ideologies I agreed with my parents on and which aspects of their worldview I thought were detrimental to achieving my goals. This took clarity of mind and the capacity to lean into said hardship. Once I was able to find this grounding, I then took the time not only to let go of these perspectives but also to grieve them. Grief was unexpected for me; I hadn't expected to need to detach myself from my conditioning in order to make internal space for new narratives to form. I was also intending to maintain a genuine respect for those who influenced me, who were now flawed individuals in my eyes. Discovering their flaws felt like a betrayal of the superhumans I had remembered from my childhood.

It was painful to reconcile the fact that my parents also got to be people, perfectly imperfect, and I needed to give myself time to feel scared, disappointed and eventually gently resigned to the fact that my superhero parents also had an everyday identity they inhabited. For all of the pity and disappointment I needed to feel towards them for a time, this process was also a part of seeing them as full-fledged humans, complete with flaws and thought processes incompatible to my own.

Once I was able to reconcile these shadows and focus on how to move forward as an individual, the positive qualities of my upbringing, such as generosity, honesty and empathy, began to flourish within me and I was able to harness them for good. Upon engaging these shiny new characteristics, I found myself skyrocketing towards the goals I had only dreamt about in that stony haze of my teenage bedroom!

My journey of understanding how my family influenced me was a process I felt I was going through in isolation. In reality, I was inviting everyone in my life into the process with me. Once I realized this, I found myself constantly starting dialogues about childhood with my peers, asking them to share their perspectives, and I discovered I wasn't alone; others also seemed to be in their own processes, wrestling with how to let go of the conditioning they received that wasn't helpful to them without losing the valuable lessons they learned growing up.

Whether you are coming from a family background you agree with or not, whether your parents were nonmonogamous or not, you are the one who inevitably has to take active control over this process. It's a very scary thing to do and may require re-engaging in past trauma; therefore I recommend doing so with professionals and those you trust to be able to hold your complexity with compassion. I am an extrovert who is most comfortable with a sprawling web of people, so I used the support network I had outside of my family, and it was the only way I was able to grow through the hardship involved to become the person I am today. This not only allowed me the benefit of having multiple avenues of support, but also provided the unexpected pleasure of having a network of people see me go through this process and bloom into adulthood of my own accord, instead of doing it in the shadow of my tribe and as who I perceived them wanting me to be.

I am proud of the person I am today, accepting all the parts of my history and identity coming together to showcase the vivacious rainbow I often present as. Through the journey of writing this book, I have been asked, "Why share your story now and not when you are older?" My flippant response is "Because I'm interesting enough to make it worthwhile!" In truth, I have felt that this story is larger than myself; it is one example, among many, of how to create love and safety, specifically for children, outside of nuclear, monogamous design.

We are living in a time of globalization, and as the world continues to expand and connect, these stories of family and tribe building need to be heard. If you have a story that you know can inspire people to find their truth and live it boldly, that story deserves to be told. As you move through your life and get the chance to influence those younger than you, help them see their power and give them the freedom to explore how it works best for them. This is youth empowerment, and it's what will help change the world into the kind of place where folks from any family background can have the chance to thrive. Which is basically the point, right?

The story of my childhood is the conversation I find myself involved in more than any other. I hope you have found useful insights in it for creating systems and practices for budding polyamorous families who will hopefully influence their children in positive ways, as much as parents can.

In the end, it's not about whether or not your family screwed you up, it's about how your family influenced you and how you use that knowledge to support your strengths, inform your decisions and guide you in building the very best life for yourself. Throughout the complex experience of my childhood, there was never a question about whether I was loved, and I know that this was a huge privilege that has carried me through the darkest parts of my life.

No matter what your own experience growing up was, you have an opportunity in your adulthood to build family and community based around this ideal. I'd like to leave with you with a blessing that my mothers never let me forget: "Baby, you are a gift, inherently valuable just as you are, and you're exactly what the world needs you to be."

Also By Thorntree Press

A World in Us

Louisa Leontiades, 2017

"As Louisa takes us on her relationship road trip, she ultimately delivers a map on how to start and continue a process of wise self-examination and relationship success."

— from the foreword by Gracie X., author of *Wide Open: My Adventures in Polyamory, Open Marriage, and Loving on My Own Terms*

Necessary to Life

Louisa Leontiades, 2017

"This is the real deal! Louisa Leontiades bares her soul to tell the whole truth about what it's really like living in an open relationship—all the joy and the heartbreak."

— Kathy Labriola, author of *Love in Abundance* and *The Jealousy Workbook*

Stories from the Polycule: Real Life in Polyamorous Families

Dr. Elisabeth Sheff, 2015

"Readers engaged in or curious about polyamorous families will find plenty to ponder in this eclectic and enlightening collection."

—*Publishers Weekly*

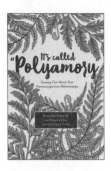

It's Called "Polyamory": Coming Out About Your Nonmonogamous Relationships

Tamara Pincus and Rebecca Hiles, 2017

"Doing poly, holding poly space in the world, is hard work, often thankless. Thanks to this wonderful resource, it's now a lot easier."

— Loraine Hutchins, co-editor, *Bi Any Other Name: Bisexual People Speak Out*

Claiming the B in LGBT: Illuminating the Bisexual Narrative

Edited by Kate Harrad, 2018

Praise for the UK edition (*Purple Prose*):
"With bisexuality becoming ever more visible in mainstream culture, this book is essential reading for bi people and would-be allies, within the LGBT community and beyond. You need a copy in your life."

— Louise Carolin, *DIVA* magazine

Love, Retold

Tikva Wolf, 2017

"A book that will blow your heart and mind into a million billion pieces, and then stitch them, so tenderly and so gracefully, back together."

— Anya Light, author of *Opening Love*

Ask Me About Polyamory!
The Best of Kimchi Cuddles

Tikva Wolf, 2016

"The warm and open style, and great way of getting complex things across simply, makes it one of the best relationship comics out there."

— Dr. Meg-John Barker, author of *Rewriting the Rules*

When Someone You Love is Polyamorous

Dr. Elisabeth Sheff, 2016

"I recommend it for anyone considering coming out to their friends and family, or anyone who has come out but is having trouble getting their loved ones to understand and accept their relationships."

— Jessica Burde, author of *Polyamory and Pregnancy*

Love's Not Color Blind

Kevin Patterson, 2018

"Love's Not Color Blind should be required reading for people who are sex positive, as well as those in alternative relationships or communities."

— Mark Michaels and Patricia Johnson, co-authors of *Designer Relationships*

It's Ok Feelings, I Got You

Tikva Wolf, 2018

In this workbook, Wolf leads you through simplified drawing exercises using events from your actual life, enabling you to take a step back and see things from a whole new angle. Using these visual activities, you can gain some helpful new tools for navigating interpersonal dynamics and getting your own needs met.

Ask: Building Consent Culture

Edited by Kitty Stryker, 2017

"There are certain conversations that deepen how you think; positively impact how you act; expand your view and understanding of the world, and forever alter how you approach it. This book is full of them. Make room for it — then spread the word."

— Alix Fox, journalist, sex educator and ambassador for the Brook sexual wellbeing charity

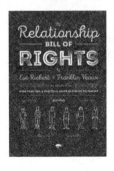

The Relationship Bill of Rights poster

Eve Rickert and Franklin Veaux, 2018

A radical framework for liberating relationships from abusive dynamics and reshaping them along principles of consent, agency, and honesty.